Will T. Hale

The First Tennessee Regiment

United States Volunteers

Will T. Hale

The First Tennessee Regiment
United States Volunteers

ISBN/EAN: 9783743314146

Manufactured in Europe, USA, Canada, Australia, Japa

Cover: Foto ©ninafisch / pixelio.de

Manufactured and distributed by brebook publishing software
(www.brebook.com)

Will T. Hale

The First Tennessee Regiment

THE FIRST TENNESSEE REGIMENT

UNITED STATES VOLUNTEERS

BEGINNING OF THE SPANISH-AMERICAN WAR

THE Anglo-Saxon stands, and for centuries has stood foremost for liberty, for the equality of men before the law, and for the fullest freedom of thought and intellectual advancement. As a result the march of the race has never been in retreat, but ever onward. It has made blunders, but it can learn a lesson, seldom committing the blunder over and over until it becomes a crime.

These conditions are reversed in Spain. That country is by nature endowed with many advantages, and yet her people are wofully down-trodden, and generally ignorant. She has made the serious mistake for long generations of trying to hold distant colonies by force of arms instead of endeavoring to bring about their contentment and prosperity. Her dealing with Cuba is an instance of her fatuous and monumental stupidity. If we entirely ignore her attitude relative to the moral and intellectual development of the Cubans, a study of the statistics of the exactments to which they have been subjected, shows the iniquity and avarice of the mother country and amply justifies the Cubans for their long continued struggle to free themselves from her grasp—a struggle seriously begun in the first of their great revolutions in 1868, and ending successfully, through the Samaritan efforts of the United States, thirty years later in the second result.

In the mind of the American people, the event which caused hostilities between this country and Spain was the destruction, on February 15, 1898, of the United States battleship Maine in Havana harbor, but the war had been coming for some time before that incident. The cruelties of the Spanish authorities toward the Cubans, hardly precedented except in the history of Spain toward the helpless peoples who have fallen under her power; the impotency exhibited by the dons in their efforts to subdue them; and the continued menace to our interests which this long drawn out contest brought about—these things inspired various resolutions in Congress looking to armed intervention. Even if the Maine had not been destroyed the war would undoubtedly have materialized. The report of the naval court appointed for the purpose of inquiring into the cause of the catastrophe, finding that the ship had been destroyed by the explosion of a mine—seeming to throw the responsibility for the crime on the Spanish government—merely hastened the conflict.

The war spirit after the report became general. "Remember the Maine!" was the slogan. Party lines were erased, and the people as one man were for war. On April 5, 1898, Consul General Fitzhugh Lee was ordered home from Havana, and to bring with him all American citizens in the Cuban capital. President McKinley sent his long expected message to Congress, asking authority to take measures to secure the termination of hostilities in Cuba, to secure in the island the establishment of a stable government, and to use the military and naval forces of the United States as might be necessary to carry out his policy. Congress acted promptly, voting a large sum to carry out the proposed measures. In anticipation of the war, the regular army was ordered to mobilize at Tampa, Mobile, New Orleans, and Chickamauga. Gen. Woodford, the American minister to Spain, was given his passports by the Spanish government. And on April 22 the American fleet under Admiral Sampson sailed from Key West to effect a blockade of Havana and the northern coast of Cuba. Then came the President's ultimatum to Spain, demanding a reply on or before noon of Saturday, April 23, and a few days afterward his proclamation calling for 125,000 troops. On a joint resolution passing through both Houses of Congress, on April 25, it was signed by President McKinley, and war was formally declared, although four days previously the first shotted gun was fired, throwing a shell from the United States gunboat Nashville across the bow of the Spanish steamer Buena Ventura, the first prize taken by our blockading fleet.

RESPONSE OF THE VOLUNTEERS

WHEN President James K. Polk, at the outbreak of the war with Mexico called for volunteers, more than 200,000 men responded at once. The response to President McKinley's proclamation was as prompt and enthusiastic. The people were not a little moved by sentiment—the desire to avenge the execution of

COL. GRACEY CHILDERS.

APPOINTED COLONEL OF THE FIRST TENNESSEE, TO SUCCEED COL. W. C. SMITH.

Crittenden and the slaughter of the crew of the ill-fated Virginia, and to put an end to the starving of noncombatting Cuban women and children; but over and above all surged the resolution to punish Spain for the insult offered to the stars and stripes on February 15, 1898. Then there was obliterated the imaginary line between North and South, sons of the Lost Cause and of the Union were actuated by the same high patriotism, and it could then be truthfully sung:

"There is a cry that rises and swells on every breeze—
No laggards on the shore and no laggards on the seas;
From homes of love and liberty the patriot souls are seen,
Thank God the land's united, the sobbing waves serene,"

And Tennessee? As had been her course since her admission into the Union in 1796, she showed by her enthusiasm her indorsement of the sentiment—"Our country, may she always be right; but—our country, right or wrong." All the States promised their quota of troops, but even as early as April 20, this telegram was sent to the papers from Washington, proving once more Tennessee's right to be called the Volunteer State.

WASHINGTON, April 20—All day today letters and telegrams have been pouring in upon Secretary of War Alger from prominent citizens of Tennessee, offering their services in the event of war. Similar telegrams have been received by the Tennessee delegation, which were duly forwarded to the war department. So far more offers have been received from Tennessee than from any other State in the Union.

Under the first call for volunteers Tennessee's quota was to be three regiments of infantry. The officers of the First were:

Colonel—Wm. Crawford Smith.

Lieutenant Colonel—Gracey Childers.

Majors—Albert B. Bayless, B. Frank Cheatham, and John G. Maguire.

Major and Surgeon—Richard A. Barr.

Captain and Assistant Surgeon—R. M. Kirby-Smith and Percy Jones.

First Lieutenant and Adjutant—James K. Polk.

First Lieutenant and Quartermaster—Andrew J. Duncan.

Captain and Chaplain—Lewis J. Leland.

The field officers of the Second were:

Colonel—Keller Anderson.

Lieutenant Colonel—Thomas E. Patterson.

Majors—Frank H. Heffley, Mark A. Walker, and George W. Seay.

Those of the Third were:

Colonel—James P. Fyffe.

Lieutenant Colonel—Daniel M. Coffman.

Majors—William Brown, James W. Meeks, and Edwin C. Ramage.

Under the second call a fourth regiment was organized, with the following field officers:

Colonel—George LeRoy Brown.

Lieutenant Colonel—Harvey H. Hannah.

Majors—William C. Tatom, William O. Vertrees, and J. Cram Epler.

Two of the regiments—the Second and Third—were discharged before they saw active service in the field, and the Fourth was quartered awhile in Cuba, then discharged. While they were not permitted to take part in any of the battles between this country and Spain or between our forces and the Filipinos, the soldiers were ready to fight like Tennesseans, and would have reflected glory on American arms.

The First Tennessee Regiment was the earliest organized, the companies constituting it being Company A, Nashville; Company B, Columbia; Company C, Nashville; Company D, Lawrenceburg; Company E, Nashville; Company F, Nashville; Company G, Waverly; Company H, Clarksville; Company I, Big Sandy; Company K, Springfield; and Companies L and M to be recruited from Nashville. On April 23 the National State Guard was ordered out, the order from Adjutant Charles Sykes being addressed to the various commanders throughout the State, and to those of the First Regiment. It was made in anticipation of the President's call. The troops were to rendezvous at Nashville preparatory to being mustered into the service by Lieut. Samuel Seay, of the Fourteenth United States Infantry. There was long the and excitement and enthusiasm then for weeks in the capital city. The regular troops were passing daily on the trams; the volunteers along the various thoroughfares recalled to mind the stirring days of 1861, and patriotism could almost be felt in the air!

At length the companies were filled, and the Tennessee troops repaired to camps outside the city limits to be drilled and to await orders to march to the front. The waiting to these heroic boys proved a sore trial, for they enlisted to fight and not to rest idly in camp. Even the Governor of the State, Hon. Robert L. Taylor, became inspired by the war spirit, and the volunteers expressed a desire that he should command them.

The Daughters of the American Revolution, through Mrs. E. C. Lewis, on May 17, 1898, presented the First Tennessee with a flag, and soon after the regiment repaired to Cherokee Park to await further orders.

ORDERED TO SAN FRANCISCO

THE order to move came in due time. Familiar scenes were to be forsaken, and the old blue skies of Tennessee were to be looked upon no more for months. In all this, despite their ardor, the Tennesseans found a trial, for it is no insignificant matter to clasp the hands of friends in farewell, perhaps for the last time, and to reflect that in distant climes there would be lacking the touch of mother's wifely, or sister's tender palm and the lovelight from loving eyes. On June 16 they folded their tents, and after an uneventful journey reached San Francisco, going into quarters at Camp

COL. GRACEY CHILDERS AND STAFF
OLD FORT IN THE BACKGROUND

Merritt. Their reception at San Francisco was gratifying in the extreme.

Camp Merritt proved an unhealthful place, however. There was an increase of maladies of acute bronchitis and other maladies which were hard to fight on account of the damp nights.

As many of the Tennessee troops had sickened and predicted, it was found necessary to seek better quarters. Camp Merriam, in a beautiful valley of the Presidio, was selected. The climatic change was at once seen to be beneficial. In a short while the sick list fell off nearly fifty per cent.

The citizens continued their good offices, and everything glided smoothly with the exception of a few acts by unruly soldiers, who, however, redeemed any mistake they made, by their valor in the Philippines.

Orders were received more than once for the First Tennessee to proceed to Manila, but were as often reconsidered. Homesickness began to take possession of many of the soldiers. As one of the officers said "they wanted Manila or home." It seemed that they were not to take any real part in the war—were not to taste any of the excitement of conflict, or to gain any of the glory of victory, not reflecting that these also serve who only stand and wait. They were Tennesseans—and the record of the Tennessee soldier is that when there is any fighting to do, he wants to take part in it.

Time had developed the fact that there were members of the regiment who were immature, physically disabled, and undesirable for other reasons, and in October an order came from Washington to have them discarged. After an inspection made by Maj. Fields, 154 men were given discharges.

In the meantime, as stated, a number of the soldiers had died in camp—none the less heroes because they did not fall in line of battle.

> Not above's duty done,
> Not a tear to glory won
> Where the storms of battle blow
> Names of those who nothing doubt
> Fame will write them in and prize
> On the tablets of the ages.

ON THE WAY TO MANILA

WHILE some of the San Francisco papers became unfriendly toward the soldiers as journeying there, on account of the scare they gave a crust in over-taxing their wrath to keep it warm until the moment when the country's defenders began leaving for Manila, the latter were not without a host of friends and well wishers. A portion of the First Regiment left on the *Zealandia*, on the evening of October 29, for Manila. The companies which embarked were A, B, C, E, F, L, and M, comprising 500 men and officers. The remaining four companies—mostly new recruits—followed one week later on the *City of Puebla*, under

the command of Lieut. Col. Gracey Childress. The wives of Chief Surgeon Richard Barr and Chaplain J. J. Leland were, by special permission of the Secretary of War, allowed to accompany their husbands. Thousands of the citizens of San Francisco were on the dock to bid them good-bye, and in this token of the esteem of the populace they forgot the harsh things said about them by the papers. They arrived at Manila in the Philippine Islands November 28, 1898.

A GLANCE AT THE PHILIPPINES

THE number of islands in the archipelago is variously estimated at from 600 to 2,000. If the Carolines and the Ladrone islands are not counted with the Philippines proper, however, there are probably about 1,200. The more important are Luzon, having 41,000 square miles; Mindanao, 37,000; Samar, 5,500; Panay, 4,600; Palawan, 4,150; Mindoro, 4,050; Leyte, 3,090; Negros, 2,300; Cebu, 1,650, and Masbate, 1,315.

The Filipinos first appeared in history in 1509, but the islands were not discovered till 1521. The conquest of the islands was accomplished by a few Spaniards in the sixteenth century, and was held by them until turned over to the United States in 1898.

The natives were driven into an insurrection in 1896, on account of the rapacity of the monks, and the revolt was directed as much against them as the Spanish government. Rents were raised so that the small farmers could not pay; they rebelled, and for the first time rich and poor, educated and ignorant, united in the common struggle against Spain. Their leader was Don Emilio Aguinaldo y Famy, who has been giving the Americans so much trouble.

The war between the Filipinos and Spaniards had been interrupted by the agreement of the Spanish government with Aguinaldo and other insurgent leaders to pay them $800,000 and introduce all the reforms for which the Filipinos had been asking. Of this money, $400,000 was paid into a bank in Hong Kong. The insurgents considered it a trust fund to be held as a guaranty of Spanish good faith. Aguinaldo began a new insurrection soon as the Spanish government failed to fulfil its promises. Nine thousand Spanish prisoners were held by his forces, and an army of 30,000 declared to be under arms. He claimed, even after the Americans had taken Manila, that he was the de facto ruler of the country, and interfered conspicuously in the administration of affairs there. Complications arose, and it was soon seen by those in a position to see that trouble was brewing between the Americans and the insurgents. The expected outbreak occurred on the night of Saturday, February 4, 1899, at Manila. Three ventures

LIEUT.-COL. ALBERT BAYLESS

some Filipinos ran past the pickets of the First Nebraska Volunteers, at Santa Mesa. They were challenged, and retired without replying. Once more they tried the experiment, and were challenged and thrust back beyond the picket line. For the third time they approached the picket line maintained by the Americans. Corporal Greely challenged them, and then opened fire, killing one and wounding another. This was the signal for the first battle between the Americans and Filipinos—a conflict which the Tennesseans foreshadowed some time before in letters to friends at home.

BEFORE referring further to the first engagement between the Americans and Filipinos a glance at the movements of the First Tennessee after its arrival in the Philippines will be given.

There have been expressions to the effect that the Tennesseans have done nothing in this war worthy of record an erroneous idea, certainly, having its inspiration in the execrable trait of humanity which gave rise to the scriptural maxim that a prophet is not without honor save in his own country. If we had no other proof of their gallantry, it would be sufficiently proved by the letter written by Gen. Otis in their praise. This letter was written February 11, 1899, to Gen. Miller, off Iloilo, and from it is taken this significant extract:

The Tennessee Regiment has done some good fighting, and should you place them on shore, will take the city of Iloilo without assistance from artillery or gunboats. They go down with enthusiasm gained here (at Manila) on the battle line, where they fought desperately.

No greater tribute could be tendered. No greater confidence could have been shown the picked marksmen at King's Mountain, the soldiers under Jackson at Horseshoe Bend or the troops who stormed and carried the City of Mexico a half century ago.

And while on this subject of dauntless intrepidity, we should not overlook two or three instances of individual courage happening during the war, which were topics for the whole people at the time of their occurrence. One was outlined in a cablegram from Manila. "Near Jaro," it read, "Sergeant Clement C. Jones of the Third Battalion, Tennessee Regiment made a dash from the outposts across eight hundred yards of open rice fields, forded a river, seized a rebel standard, and returned unscathed with his trophy, through a hail of Mauser bullets from the Filipino intrenchments." Collier's Weekly, giving an illustration of the thrilling act, declares that it was the most desperate deed of daring the war has pro-

duced. Another was during a skirmish at September near Naga, Island of Cebu, when Lewis Burns displayed laudable heroism. This incident is best given in the language of Lucian Williams, a Tennessee soldier:

"We all marched up into the town," he wrote in a private letter, the place mentioned being Manticao. Finding it deserted, we put out our sentinels and spent the night in a convent. At about six next morning four shots were heard, and our native soldiers reported the insurgents advancing on the town. In a few moments we had on our equipment, and were advancing in the direction of the shots, our fighting force being 37 Americans and about 100 natives, 7 of the latter being armed with American made guns, the rest with spears.

"When we had gone but a short distance from quarters, the captain ordered me to take one man and guard quarters. I had spent hardly two hours keeping men, weeping women and children out of quarters when here came our boys back, and to my surprise and horror the detachment was headed by four men carrying a stretcher with an American soldier cold in death. Then came another stretcher bearing a wounded man shot through the stomach. Then came a second corpse, my friend Adams, with a horrible gash out of his half-opened eyes, showing he had died hard. Then a native fatally wounded and five men slightly wounded. Then another of our boys slightly wounded, another with his canteen shot to pieces, and still another with his bayonet bent with a bullet. Last of all came my old friend, Lewis Burns, bent down under seven guns and three pairs of bloody sidearms. He explained it all to me.

"They advanced along a road running parallel with the bay, built on an embankment some eight feet high, with water on both sides at high tide. About a mile down the road the water ceases on the landward side of the road and a bluff fourty feet high rises, on the top of which the insurgents had their fort, built of rock, almost over the road.

"The boys advanced, firing into this, but received no return fire and had gotten right under it, intending to climb up and take it, when a perfect shower of stones, bullets, and other missiles came from this cut now planted at each end and from the Remingtons and Mausers, killing one man and wounding half a dozen more.

"Capt. Walker, cool and deliberate, ordered the men to give it to them, but finding his fire ineffective and that longer delay meant the death of perhaps his whole force, ordered retreat. However, one man was killed and several wounded of his little force was gained.

"In the midst of the most trying time and most galling fire, Lewis Burns, one of our Nashville boys, jumped down the bank, amid retreat and fire, and took hold of one of his fallen comrades, stood calling for assistance. And by the way of parenthesis, will say, he will soon be made a corporal, promoted for bravery on the field.

Before a month had passed after the arrival of Col. Smith and his Tennessee regiment at Manila, that officer began attracting the attention of his superiors. He was accordingly advanced by Gen. Otis to an independent command. He was assigned to the command of Cavite, and of all the troops stationed there.

Writing to Maj. E. C. Lewis of Nashville under date of January 12, 1899, he said:

"I have one of the battalions (Cheatham's) from

MAJ. B. FRANK CHEATHAM.
NOW SENIOR MAJOR THIRTY-SEVENTH U. S. V.

my own regiment, the battalion of the First California Heavy Artillery, the Wyoming battalion of infantry, Troop A of the Nevada cavalry, and Battery A of the Wyoming Light Artillery, including my headquarters' staff and band—in all about 1,200 men, and still being in command of the First and Third Battalions of my own regiment at Manila, this makes about 1,800 men I have to look after. Lieut. Col. Childers is in immediate command of the First and Third Battalions, which are reported, of course, from my headquarters as detached and stationed at Manila.

Col. Smith was ordered to Cavite to relieve Col. D. D. Van Valzah, of the Eighteenth United States Infantry, who was designated for service in another section of the Philippine Islands. Cavite, to be specific, is eight miles from Manila across the bay, or twenty miles around by land.

The soldiers were not idle from their arrival. It was claimed that the members of the First had been kept largely in the rear, to restore order in the territory taken by our troops, but this is a mistake. Lieut. James K. Polk is authority for the correction, and he also says that they had not done any police duty up to June 24, 1899. "The regiment," he stated in a communication to the Nashville American, "has done outpost duty continuously, each company being on such duty from once in two days to once in four days. These outposts are located along the Jaro river on one side, and between Iloilo river and the bay on the other. Along the lines we have built small blockhouses to protect the men from the weather and bullets, and for the first two months after we reached Manila, scarcely a day passed in which there were not small outpost skirmishes."

Circumstances and opportunities bring out the best qualities of soldier and civilian. Dewey had long been in the navy. It required the war with Spain to show that he was a bulldog fighter. Lee had been for years in the army; it needed the exigencies of a great conflict to prove that he was the leading general of his time. If circumstances had not intervened, neither of these heroes would have won his reputation. So with the First Tennessee. Placed at the front, in the storm of shot and shell, it would have been heralded from the beginning of hostilities and made as famous as any regiment in the battles around Santiago.

As shown, they were kept at Nashville and San Francisco for something near half a year. Arriving at Manila, weeks passed before they were given an opportunity to show their fighting qualities. Of course no criticism should be made relative to the forced inactivity of the regiment, the only Southern regiment in the Philippines, by the way. Gen. Otis was supposed to know his duty. It was plain enough, however, that "the boys" were not underestimated, even by the general himself. His actions toward Col. Smith, as well as his letter to Gen. Miller, mentioned elsewhere, abundantly prove this.

But a time was approaching when the soldiers could show their spirit and receive the eulogy of the public.

This was first demonstrated at Manila, in the attack made by the Filipinos.

THE FIRST AT MANILA

MENTION has been made of the opening clash between the Americans and insurgents on February 4, 1899. The continuous battles around Manila were furious and bloody, the loss to the enemy being several thousand.

All the reports of any length testified to the desperate bravery exhibited by the First Tennessee. The regiment simply covered itself with glory. The Second Battalion, Col. Smith and staff, had been ordered back from Cavite only a few days before, doubtless in anticipation of some kind of trouble. Perhaps a better idea of the conflict and the part the Tennessee troops took can be given by quoting from the letters of eye-witnesses. In a communication to the Banner, Lieut. Winston Pitcher says:

"Sunday night, Lieut. Col. Childers and Maj. Maguire came in on a run from the city, and said there was firing on the outposts out on the waterworks road, where the Nebraskans were. About that time an aide dashed up, and in about two minutes Chief Bugler Embry was sounding 'To arms!' The men gave a wild yell of delight, and rushed into their tents after arms. The regiment formed in the San Lucia road and waited for orders, and I, with thirty men, was left to guard the rag boxes and tents. Presently the regiment moved off, and I made an exultation to the stars! All night long I stood out on the river front and listened. The sound of firing came in from every point except the bay. And it came from there, too, for the Monadnock and the Charleston were shelling the woods. I am not out on a still hunt for a hero's death, but I wanted to be with the regiment.

"About 8 o'clock Sunday morning the regiment came plodding back, and every individual man was saying something that was not nice. They had been marched to the other side of the walled city, and had stayed there all night. At 8 o'clock I was relieved, and as I was going toward my tent (the firing had never ceased) I met an aide. To my query, 'What news?' he said: 'I'm going to send your Second Battalion to help out the Nebraskans.' I broke into a run, and by the time the order to get ready came the battalion was ready to march, and the First and Third tearing their hair.

"Manila is a much larger city than I thought. We marched five miles, and were still in town. As we passed the various barracks, those left behind yelled, 'Give 'em h—l for us, boys!' We were nearly out of the city, and were standing in columns of fours, when we heard our first Mausers. About a peck of them ripped through a bamboo hedge and—well, no living being can know what they sounded like unless he could hear them coming. It is demoralizing.

"What we halted for was not long in coming. An artillery officer dashed back and ordered up the litter bearers, saying the colonel was killed. I did not know Colonel Smith was with us, and when I ran to the front of the column and saw the gallant old gentleman lying in the road, I was horribly shocked. Adjutant Polk, Maj. Cheatham, and Surgeon Kirby-Smith were bending over him. He had fallen just as he turned into the road under fire, and we all thought he was shot until late in the day. The word was passed down the line, and the men began to

MAJ JOHN A MAGUIRE
MAJ W J WHITTHORNE

MAJ A C GILLEM

swear and demand an advance, for they wanted revenge. The knightly old gentleman was carried to the rear, and the word forward was given.

"The colonel was in the act of giving Maj. Cheatham his instructions when he fell, and, outside of a general idea of the work to be done he knew nothing. We were to support the Utah Battery, which was hammering away 2,000 yards ahead. We had to cross the San Juan river on a high-backed bridge, the most exposed place on the firing line, and the only way was in a column of forty-five. The gallant little Cheatham never hesitated, but ordered us forward. The Mausers, thank goodness, all fired high, were whirring, and the men were looking at each other as they marched along, when, just at the right moment somebody yelled, 'Charge.' It was like new whisky. Every man threw up his head, gave a yell, and then began a footrace in perfect order. We went over the bridge, dashed into position behind the battery, and in less time than it takes to tell it Companies B and M were sending niggers to glory. We drove them back slowly, for they were brave little devils, and if they knew how to shoot we wouldn't be here to tell about it. We edged along, running them out of trench after trench, until we took the hill—which, by the way, is called San Juan.

"The Nebraskans, who had been fighting thirty hours, were on our left, and had the bulk of the fighting. They lost several men in this advance. We rested awhile at the insurgent headquarters, then formed a long line and attacked the San Phillips convent, which is practically impregnable; but we had little trouble, as the yellow boys had been hit too hard on the hill. The campaign the rest of the day took on the form of a rabbit drive. They would lie in ambush and shoot a few rounds, and would be dropped by our marksmen when they tried to get away. I hear we drove several hundred across the river, and saw more dead ones than I care to think of. We spent the night in the convent.

"The Tennessee troops did not seem to have even a little shyness nor excitement. They laughed, and most remarkable of all, preserved perfect fire discipline. My company, I know, never fired a shot without orders, and the officers of the others say the same. The only trouble was keeping some of the men behind the line, they were so anxious to see and do something. John Bass, the celebrated war correspondent, who is doing the campaign for Harper's Weekly, was with us all day. He said nothing for quite awhile, but finally told me he never saw such coolness and discipline. He told me confidentially that he was betting on our going to pieces when we crossed the bridge, but he now knew the men would go anywhere. He was surprised at the shooting, for we killed some on the run at 2,000 yards.

"Some one asked Maj. Cheatham who had shown the best nerve. He replied that there was no best, that he had watched every one, and if he was asked to recommend a man for the bravest he would have to send the battalion, as they all looked alike to him."

Another account was given by Lieut. Robert Milam, in a letter to his father, who resides in Nashville:

"We went with the determination," he wrote, "to carry honor to Dixie or die in the attempt. We came up on the Fourth Cavalry at the end of a lane, and right here I want to say that I never saw men who feared death less than the boys under their first fire. The bullets were flying over our heads and cutting down leaves all around us. In going up this lane the boys were joking with each other about it. I didn't see a single man who faltered. Well, we halted in the rear of the Fourth Cavalry, and decided that the best plan would be for us to flank them while the Fourth held their fire in front, and we set about it accordingly.

"We cut through the trees to our left and darted across, one at a time, an open space that the sharpshooters were working on, and gained blockhouse 13. From here we formed the skirmish line and advanced across the rice fields towards the woods where the Filipinos were. This advance was made in rushes of about fifty yards, and then halted, lying down. Here was where the Mausers played 'Home, Sweet Home' to us. We then swung our line into the right a little, and the Fourth opened at the same time, and also a part of the Third Artillery. The Filipinos had by this time seen our men and retreated, and then broke into a run, and finally scattered like a disorganized mob.

"It was all we could do to restrain the men. We followed them for about three miles, and had to give it up as night came on and we were in danger of getting cut off from the trenches, and ammunition was low. We relieved the Fourth at the trenches that night, and nothing occurred, outside of a little ragged firing, of any consequence the rest of the night. I forgot to tell you that we did not go out as a regiment, but the battalions were sent separately to different places. The Second Battalion did the heaviest fighting, as the natives made a good stand for a while.

"They were sent to reinforce the Utah Battery and Idaho Volunteers, and were ordered to take a bridge held by the natives.

"The charge was made; they gave the rebel yell, and poured in such a galling fire that the niggers couldn't stand it, and turned tail. They took the bridge and fought their way to the waterworks, two miles further on, and took them also. Capt. Whitthorne was slightly wounded in the arm. This is all the facts I could find out.

"Col. Smith died of apoplexy. The Third Battalion did not get into anything as they were used as a reserve. The most remarkable thing of all is that we were all under fire from one to five hours, and under from eight to fifteen hours' scattering fire and not a man lost. We killed, wounded, and captured more than 2,000 Filipinos. So far as can be known, our losses are 115 killed and wounded badly; these will die—and over 200 slightly wounded. The Fourteenth United States Infantry lost more than any other regiment."

As stated in Lieutenant Milam's letter, the battalions comprising the Tennessee companies were sent to different places. To be more precise, on February 5, Col. Smith, with Cheatham's battalion, was sent to the Santa Mesa district, where they were on the fighting line until the following evening. On the same day Col. Childers, with Bayless' battalion, was ordered to the Paco district, and he commanded on the left of the line at the taking of blockhouse No. 11 and in the pursuit of the insurgents afterwards, while Maguire's battalion was sent to the Tondo district, and served on that part of the line. The whole regiment was returned to camp after the battle of February 6, and ordered to prepare for going on board ship.

The members of the First won glory enough in the affairs around Manila, but the death of Col. Smith cast a gloom over them. He was a capable officer, was loved by his men, and would have greatly distinguished himself had he not fallen so early in the engagement, a victim of apoplexy.

It may as well be stated here as further about

CAPT NICK K GIVENS.
CAPT GASTON O'BRIEN.   LIEUT T H BATES.   CAPT H B MYERS.

that Lieut. Col. Tracey Childers succeeded to the command left vacant by the death of Col. Smith. Promotions followed, so that the roster of commissioned officers was radically changed, as will be seen by a reference to the pages following this sketch.

THE TENNESSEANS AT ILOILO

O N the night of February 10, the First Tennessee arrived off Iloilo, in the Isle of Panay, where conditions were much like those at Manila and where Gen. Miller had been waiting for weeks in the harbor; and on the morning of February 11, although the last regiment ordered ashore, it was the first to make a landing.

The insurgents protested against the landing of the Americans, consequently the place was bombarded. A 6-pounder thundered from the *Petrel*, and the city was immediately set on fire by the natives. Then followed other shells from the *Petrel* and the *Charleston*. A party of sailors and a portion of the First effected a landing, beating the Eighteenth Regulars ashore. They landed from small boats, jumping into the surf, and wading. Rushing into the city, fighting as they went, they succeeded in saving a part of it from the flames. "After the fire died down," wrote a Tennessee boy, "the scene along the beach was awful. Bodies of dogs, cats, horses, and a few men and women were lying here and there; some burned, others killed by shells and bullets. Spanish families standing here and there, weeping over the ruins of their homes, but greeting us with smiles, their streaming eyes begging us to take vengeance. We took it. We are holding down a firing line four miles long (two regiments and a battery of artillery. We may have another fight, but I doubt it, though we are occasionally worried by sharpshooters. Two regulars were killed over the river by sharpshooters over a mile away."

The following is an extract from Lieut. Col. A. H. Bayless' account of the way the First occupied its time from the taking of Iloilo to about June 1:

"Since the taking of Iloilo our regiment, or detachments of the regiment, have taken part in all battles or skirmishes that have taken place here, and if you are not too weary, I will give you a short account of what has happened since February 11.

"On the morning of February 25, four of our companies marched to Mandurrao, which is located between Molo and Jaro, and in a direct line between these two cities, but some distance further into the interior. While the command was resting, Lieut. Milam was sent out in charge of a scouting party and in about an hour one of the scouts returned and reported that the enemy had been located about one and a half miles out. Two companies were sent up the road and two made a direct attack on the insurgents, who were found to be occupying three lines of trenches. Without going into details, the insurgents were driven out of their strongholds with many casualties in their own ranks, while our troops suffered none whatever. While in this case as in every battle our regiment has been in, each and every officer and man did his part well, however, the circumstances in this particular battle were more favorable for Capt. Hogan (Company E) and his company, and Lieut. Milam and his scouts from Company C, to do most of the work.

"Shortly afterwards we returned to Mandurrao, remaining there until after noon, when we returned to our barracks via Jaro.

"On March 16, the battle of Jaro river was fought, principally by Maj. Keller's battalion. However, two other companies of the Eighteenth, as well as B, C, L and M, of our regiment, participated. Our battalion was first intended as a reserve to the Eighteenth, but, as luck would have it, the insurgents were somewhat loath to retire. Therefore, Gen. Miller ordered our battalion into the firing line, and, as usual, they behaved only as you would have them. Only two of our men were scratched, and these did not even go on sick report the next morning. Some had their gun stocks shattered. One man in Company C had his hair parted 'Sam Jones' style by a Mauser bullet, it passing through his hat exactly in the center.

"On April 4 we had quite an excursion to Otan, which is up the beach about eight or nine miles from Iloilo. Three companies, under Cheatham, were placed aboard tugs and sent to a point one and a half miles above Otan, while I, with three companies, accompanied by Capt. Bridgman and a platoon of artillery, went overland. I have no hesitancy in stating that the plans mapped out by Col. Childers were most admirably executed. Cheatham and myself connecting at the exact time appointed, and swooping down upon the town of Jaro, to the utter dismay of the inhabitants. However, the insurgent army had vacated the day before. The trip, although unsuccessful in its main reasons, was successful, as we captured telegrams, letters, documents, maps, etc., which afterwards proved beneficial to our commanding general of this district. We returned to our barracks, tired and dusty, in time for dinner.

"On April 17, I went to Manila on board the Petrel, which was convoying thirteen gunboats bought from Spain, was used royally treated by all the officers, and enjoyed the trip immensely. It has always been my desire to be aboard a man-of-war in time of action, and my desire came very near being gratified, and in a manner, it was, for the reason that one of these Spanish gunboats—which by the way, were manned by the insurgents—tried to give us the shake and started off at full speed in the opposite direction. No sooner had the quartermaster reported this and to the officer of the deck when call to quarters was sounded, and in a very short time the Spaniard brought the runaway alongside our boat.

"In Iloilo, at the present time, we are only holding our lines, making no advances whatever, as such are our orders. The work is not as hard as the active campaigning would lead us to expect in this country at this season of the year, but at the same time it is very tiresome and irksome to be doing as we are, as longs to get out and have a good rabbit hunt."

As the fighting around Iloilo about the middle of March, referred to in Lieut. Col. Bayless' letter, was severe, the account of the New York Herald will be appreciated. The dispatch to that journal stated:

"A battalion of the Eighteenth Infantry, a platoon of the Sixth Artillery and the machine gun battery made a reconnaissance in the direction of Mandurrao and Santa Barbara, Thursday. While they were returning the insurgents attacked the outpost on the right. Although attacked from ambush in the

BUGLE CORPS OF THE FIRST TENNESSEE REGIMENT.

broiling sun for two hours, the entire command proceeded to the assistance of their comrades, the artillery pouring shell and shrapnel upon the insurgents, who were strongly intrenched in large numbers.

"Companies C, H, and K, of the Eighteenth, deployed to the right, driving the insurgents back, and then wheeling to the left, made a junction with Companies E and I. A heavy engagement ensued. Companies B, C, M, and I, of the Tennessee Volunteers, Maj. Cheatham commanding, arrived later and formed on the left, and two more companies of the Eighteenth marched from Iloilo to act as support to the other troops. Col. Van Valzah and Maj. Keller commanded the battalions of the Eighteenth Regiment.

"Gen. Miller was on the scene early, and directed the operations from immediately behind the fighting line. He had several narrow escapes.

"The line advanced by rushes 3,000 yards under a hot fire, pouring in deliberate volleys upon the enemy's position, the artillery making good practice.

"By the time the forces were within 300 yards of the enemy's final position, darkness fell, preventing the charge, for which the Tennessee men and the companies of the Eighteenth on the right had already prepared by fixing bayonets. The retirement upon Jaro was accomplished in good order.

"The engagement was brought on by the persistent attacks upon the outpost at Jaro bridge. Nothing could be gained by forcing the enemy further back, as it was impossible, with the limited number of troops, to hold the position.

"The American troops were exhausted by the fighting and having to wade knee deep through the rice fields and sugar cane. There were several cases of prostration by the heat.

"The severity of the engagement may be judged from the fact that the Eighteenth Regiment alone fired 62,800 rounds. It is estimated that the insurgents, with their more than 2,000 rifles, fired more than double our total ammunition.

"It is impossible to tell accurately the insurgents' losses, as the American troops converged at a given point without traversing the ground shot over, but on the day after the battle I could see from Jaro belfry the enemy carting away the dead. The minimum estimate of their losses is 200 killed and 300 wounded.

"The evolutions were prettily executed and the highest credit is due the battalion and company commanders. The men are chafing at being robbed of the fruits of their victory. A charge would probably have resulted in the capture of the enemy's arms and ammunition, but from the configuration of the ground and the position of our troops, it was impossible to allow an advance in the darkness. The behavior of the troops was admirable."

...SCOUTING...
CEBU, PARDO, AND OTHER POINTS

THE soldiers of the First saw considerable service in detached companies after the taking of Iloilo, but the excitement—with the exception of that experienced in the battle described by the New York Herald correspondent—was not great.

Under date of June 28, the correspondent of the Nashville Banner wrote that Company H was at Pardo, Cebu. The detachment was with Company M, Twenty-third Regular Infantry, all under the command of Capt. W. H. Allaire. A month later Jno. Duckworth, the American correspondent, gave the information that four companies of the regiment—A, C, H, and K—were in Cebu, 300 miles south of Iloilo, having left the latter city on June 15. Still later, September 17, Lieut. Pilcher informed the Banner readers that Companies A, B and C were at Pasig, while Company G was at Taguig. They were certainly moving sufficiently among new scenes to keep their minds off of home, but the rumors which began to be heard aroused the feeling of home-sickness once more. What should we expect, then, under the circumstances, but to find Lieut. Pilcher's communication ending with somewhat of sentiment?

"Yes, the old regiment is going home," he says. "But you give them a good time, and ring the bells long enough for those to hear who are left behind. The regiment has contributed its share of those who are 'absent, but accounted for.' Every stopping place has its little squad of Tennesseans who have heard the soldiers' last tattoo. Presidio cemetery, Peru cemetery, and the Protestant cemetery, at Iloilo, all hold members of the light-hearted crowd of boys who left the State with yells and cheers over a year ago. Don't forget them. The number will be increased before this little disturbance is over, for 200 of the boys have stayed behind because they are needed, and all of them are not going back."

THE HOME-COMING
AND SOME EULOGIES

AFTER about sixteen months' absence, the First Tennessee was to return. The brief chronicles herein give only a hint of what they accomplished in those months, and what they underwent. Could the imagination do justice to those soldiers who left home with its comforts and loved ones to offer their lives on the altar of their country—were we enabled to feel all they have felt and comprehend the contests they have had with death, and stared him down—we would be willing to make their home-coming the occasion for an even grander demonstration.

The definite announcement of the return of the First Regiment was made in a dispatch from Manila, under date of October 7. The advices read as follows:

"The Tennessee Regiment, the last of the volunteer corps, will sail for the United States to-morrow, on board the transport Indiana, after a week passed in the harbor. Most of the year these troops have been stationed in the southern island. Their colonel says they are in excellent health, and have been much weakened by service. Six hundred and seventy-three will sail. Three officers and ninety-one men remain to enter into business here. Sixteen

1 CAPT SHEFFIELD CLARK   2 CAPT S O MURPHY
3 CAPT NICK GIVENS   4 CAPT VAN LEER   5 CAPT W J GILBREATH
6 CAPT GASTON O'BRIEN   7 CAPT H R RICHMOND

officers and 143 men have been discharged for re-enlistment. Two men were killed in action, and one killed accidentally. Chaplain Leland and seven men died of disease.

But here is another incident of patriotism which adds additional glory to their career: The *Indiana* was sent south early in September to collect the regiment, detachments of which were in Iloilo and Cebu. A portion were picked up at the former city. Proceeding to Cebu, it was learned that the insurgents had gathered in force among the mountains near that city; whereupon the regiment volunteered and were accepted to assist in driving the enemy from their stronghold. Here was the supreme act of valor. Beyond seas were their homes, dotting vale and dell and along city thoroughfares: they could see eyes anxiously scanning the papers, hoping to learn that they were coming back; they knew that parents' prayers were continually ascending to heaven for their safety. On the other hand, they saw an enemy of the country threatening the flag—and then they faced death once more for "Old Glory." "The President said that whenever he thought of those brave boys, he felt a lump in his throat and could hardly speak," reported a local paper detailing the visit of the Tennessee delegation to solicit his presence at Nashville on the regiment's return. How could he have been affected otherwise? And it was eminently proper that the Manila American should refer to them in these eulogistic words:

"When the First Tennessee Infantry sailed from Iloilo for Cebu the soldiers of this famous regiment thought that their fighting in the Philippines had been done. But when they arrived in Cebu and learned that an engagement was about to take place, the Tennesseans eagerly volunteered to go against the enemy. Several of the companies had turned to their shelter tents and other equipage, but all they wanted was their rifles and plenty of ammunition. Krag-Jorgensen rifles were issued to the men of the First Tennessee Infantry, but no soldier knew better how to use their old Springfields.

"The country was very rough; in fact, it was all ravines and ridges, except for one narrow and very beautiful little valley. On the mountain spurs which run down towards the sea, the insurrectos had erected a chain of forts, stretching around a semicircle and commanding every avenue of approach.

"On an elevated knob, about 2,500 yards from the rebel works, a 3 2-10 gun belonging to Light Battery G of the Sixth Artillery had been planted. The hillside was so steep the cannon was gotten into position only with the greatest difficulty. At first carabaos were made use of to drag up the gun, but when they came to the steep places the clumsy beasts were useless, and the gun was pulled up the sharp ascent by a company of soldiers. All this had been done before the Tennessee regiment arrived, and when the necessary disposition had been made all was in readiness for an attack.

"The attacking forces moved on the insurgent front in three columns.

"The first column went to the left, and was led by Maj. Maguire. It consisted of the First Battalion of the First Tennessee Infantry and detachments from the Sixth Infantry.

"In the second column, which occupied the centre, was the Second Battalion of the Tennessee Regiment and Company K of the Nineteenth Infantry. This

column was under the command of Maj. Whitthorne, an officer who formerly served with great distinction in the Confederate Army.

The third column was made up of the Third Battalion of the First Tennessee Infantry and more troops from the Twenty-third Infantry. This column inclined toward the right to create a diversion and was under the command of Maj. Gillis. Col. Childers, the commanding officer of the First Tennessee Regiment, was with the second column, and Brig.-Gen. Snyder posted himself with artillery, where he could overlook the whole field and direct the fighting to the best advantage.

"In moving forward the Americans went up the ridges, which ran somewhat parallel to one another from the seashore back to the mountains. After some well-directed shells from the lone cannon on the hilltop had been planted in the insurrecto trenches, the three columns advanced under a fierce fire from the insurgent earthworks on the mountain sides above. This was on the afternoon of September 22. The troops under Maj. Maguire encountered the fiercest resistance, and inasmuch as the lay of the country deprived this portion of the attacking force of the assistance of the other two columns, the men under the gallant Maj. Maguire had a very hard time of it. But they kept cool and stuck to their work until nightfall. Although they were fighting side by side, the Tennesseans seemed to be more lucky than their companions of the Sixth infantry. None of the Tennessee boys were hit, but out of the Sixth Infantry there were one killed and six wounded. The side hills were so very steep that the wounded men were carried back with the utmost difficulty. The soldiers who were bearing away their dead comrade slipped and fell, and the body rolled down hill 200 yards before it stopped.

"The Americans, who slept on their arms that night anchored themselves before they went to sleep. Most of the men drove their bayonets into the ground and then tied themselves to the shank, to keep from sliding down hill.

"Early the next morning the advance was resumed, and at this time the Americans were under fire from three different points. Sheltering themselves as best they could, they crawled forward up the rugged declivities and poured a deadly stream of lead into the insurrecto lines. Just as the worst of the struggle seemed about to begin, when no one doubted but what a desperate assault would have to be made in order to take the insurrecto works, the insurgents vamoosed.

"Among the trophies which the First Tennessee captured at the battle of Cebu was an insurgent battle flag, and the regiment also took the insurrecto arsenal. This was located back of the forts, and here the rebels had been manufacturing brass and zinc shells for their smooth-bore cannon. These shells were peculiar-looking things, being plugged with wood and filled with old scrap iron.

"The insurgents suffered severely from the shells thrown by the cannon on the knob, and bullets from Springfield and Krag-Jorgensen rifles laid many an insurrecto low.

"Numerous newly made graves were found in the rear of the fort, and in a shanty near which the insurgents did not have time to take away with them were found the remains of a Filipino who came in contact with a 2 10-inch shell.

"The capture of the numerous fortifications at Cebu was one of the most brilliant things that have been done in the Philippine Islands, and of all the troops who participated in the event are entitled to the greatest credit. Of the detachment of the Sixth Artillery and of the men of the Sixth, Nineteenth, and Twenty-third Infantry, the Tennesseans speak in terms of the highest praise, and the best of good feeling pre-

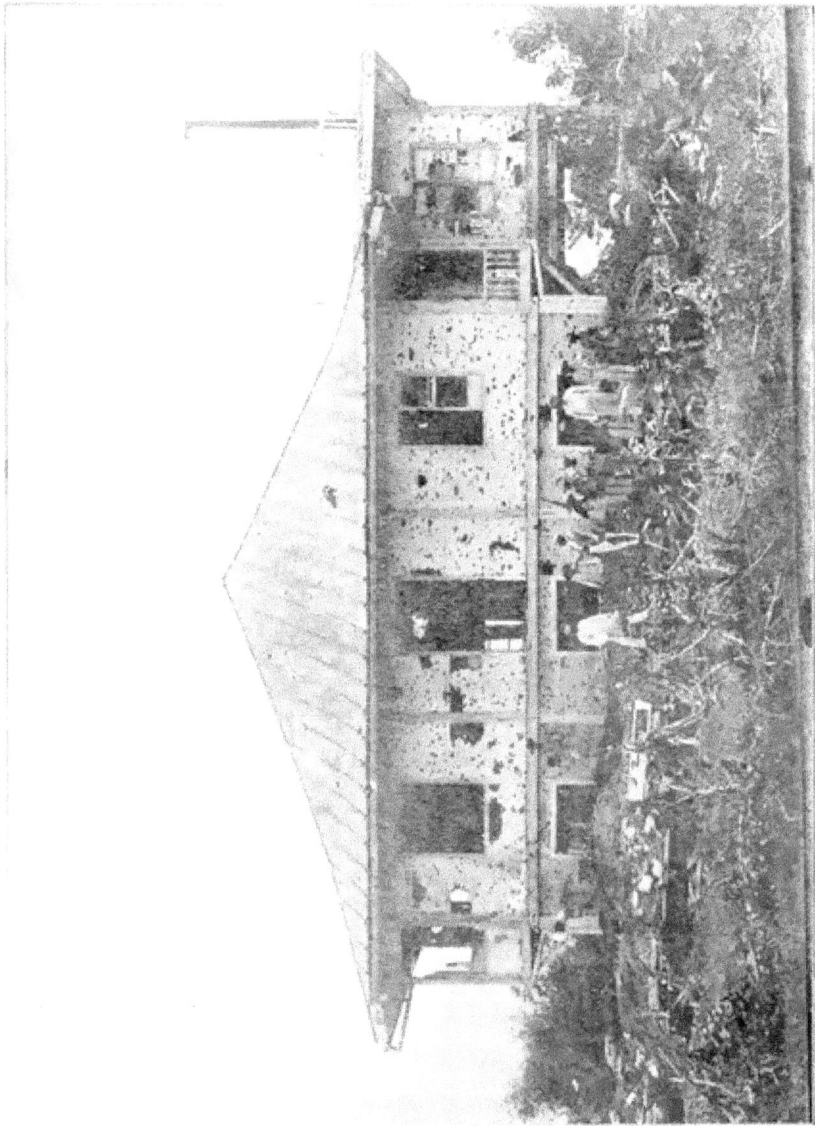

A RESIDENCE IN MALATE, SUBURB OF MANILA.
"PEPPERED" BY DEWEY IN AIDING THE FIRST LAND BATTLE AT MANILA

ARRIVAL AT SAN FRANCISCO

IN THE SUBURBS OF MANILA, SELLING BUFFALO MILK.

LINE AND STAFF OFFICERS SECOND BATTALION, CAMP MERRITT, CAL.

PROGRAMME

1. Music, "Columbia."
2. Prayer.   .   Bishop T. F. Gailor.
3. Music, "Suwanee River."
4. Address on behalf of State, Governor McMillin.
5. Address on behalf of city, . Hon. J. M. Head.
6. Address on behalf of all soldiers in this and
     former wars.   .   Hon. Tully Brown.
7. Music, "America."
8. Address,   .   .   President McKinley.
9. Music, "Stars and Stripes Forever." . Sousa.
10. Response on behalf of the First Tennessee
     Regiment.   .   .   Colonel Childers.
11. Addresses by distinguished guests, interspersed
     with music of patriotic airs.
12. Music, "Star Spangled Banner."
13. Benediction,   .   Dr. J. I. Vance.
14. Music.

AT CAMP BOB TAYLOR, NEAR NASHVILLE, JUNE, 1898.

REGIMENTAL ROSTER

COLONEL   GRACEY CHILDERS

LIEUTENANT COLONEL,	ALBERT BAYLESS	CHAPLAIN,	FRANK M. WELLS
MAJOR,	JOHN A. MAGUIRE	1ST LIEUT. AND ADJT.,	B. NELSON COFFMAN
MAJOR,	WM. J. WHITTHORNE	2D LIEUT. AND QUAR.,	JAMES W. MOORE
MAJOR,	ALVIN C. GILLEM	SERGEANT MAJOR,	M. G. CAMPBELL
MAJOR AND SURGEON,	RICHARD A. BARR	QUARTERMASTER SERGEANT,	W. N. MAGUIRE

CHAPLAIN LELAND.

COMPANY A.

George Reed, Captain.

W. A. Alexander, First Lieutenant.

J. E. Kuntz, Second Lieutenant.

Charles McKoster, former Second Lieutenant, was made First Lieutenant in Cheatham's battalion, Thirty-seventh Infantry. J. W. Burks, Jr., formerly Duty Sergeant of this company, was made Second Lieutenant of Company H. William Caruthers, former Corporal, was made First Lieutenant of Company L.

Noncommissioned Officers and Privates.

Anderson, C.	Lamberson, A. B.
Burks, J. W., Jr.	Ligon, W.
Bashaw, Lex.	Lilchens, J.
Bean, W. O.	Majors, B. K.
Bowers, R. H.	McDonald, R.
Bowers, L.	Norton, W.
Bruce, Sam.	Osborn, C. P.
Campbell, V. G.	Parker, J. R.
Campbell, W. D.	Penny, L. K.
Cockrill, D. S.	Pettrie, T. B.
Coldiron, D. F.	Petty, T. J.
Cook, J. C.	Pierce, M. J.
Cunningham, C. C.	Polk, Jas. K., Jr.
Dean, J. F.	Polk, L.
Duff, Charles.	Ramey, F.
De Ross, N. G.	Rawley, M. J.
Farr, J. C.	Shofner, Earl P.
Felber, Alfred.	Shriver, J.
Garner, H.	Skelly, J. P.
Goodloe, H.	Steele, B.
Green, Eddie	Tanksley, J. W.
Green, Thos.	Taylor, W.
Hassell, M. H.	Town, H. J.
Herron, W. A.	Turner, J.
Higgins, C.	Whittle, S.
Jones, Homer.	Wilson, Thos.
Key, G. R.	Weaser, F.
Keeton, L.	Woods, J. W.
King, E. M.	Whitley, F.
Laconby, J. W.	Zellner, J. E.

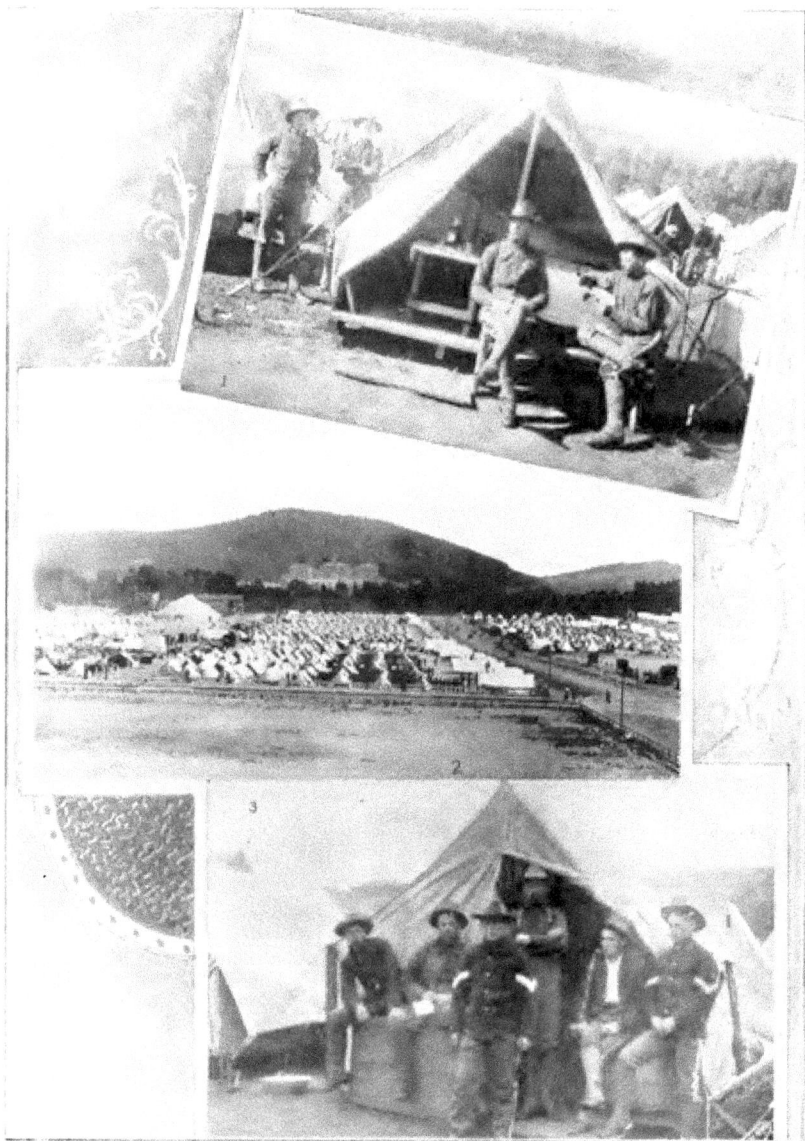

1 SCENES IN CAMP AT SAN FRANCISCO   2 THE CALIFORNIA SAND HILLS, GOLDEN GATE BEYOND
3 IN FRONT OF TENT OF LIEUT. PATRICK STACKER

GETTING THEIR COIN.

COMPANY B.

Robert Milam, Captain.

Austin Calder, First Lieutenant.

W. J. Whitthorne, former Captain, is now Major of the regiment. Edward S. Fowler, former First Lieutenant, is now practicing law in San Francisco. Robert O. Ragsdale, former Second Lieutenant, was promoted to First Lieutenant, and then transferred to the Thirty-seventh Infantry. Alvin Beskette, former First Sergeant of Company F, was made Second Lieutenant in Company B in Ragsdale's place. He was afterward transferred to the Thirty-seventh Infantry.

Noncommissioned Officers and Privates.

Allen, J. B.	Long, J. F.
Baker, Joe.	Lowthrop, W. M.
Barker, A. A.	Lunn, J. R.
Baugh, M. G.	McConnell, Ben.
Blackman, E. C.	Martin, W. T.
Boone, Jesse J.	Morgan, W. H.
Bowen, A.	Murfree, J. B.
Bullock, C. E.	Murphy, L. W.
Bunch, Chas.	Parham, W. P.
Cooper, J. O.	Pond, L. K.
Criswell, J. W.	Powell, W. E.
Darrach, T. D.	Robertson, C. B.
Ferris, R. E.	Roberts, F. B.
Fowler, O. L.	Russ, G. H.
Gaylord, G. C.	Searcy, G. W.
Glenn, O. E.	Sexton, Walter.
Gum, John H.	Smith, T. M.
Higley, Guy.	Thompson, O. L.
Hood, J. L.	Vaughan, R. T.
Holt, J. O.	Vaughan, W. T.
Jarrett, Thos.	Wade, D. F.
Lane, R. M.	Waggoner, Morton.

Waters, Wm.   Wilson, J. G.
Whittaker, Percy R.

COMPANY C.

Alfred J. Law, Captain.

Robert E. Martin, First Lieutenant.

James T. Quarles, Second Lieutenant.

Henry R. Richmond, former Captain, was transferred to the Thirty-seventh Infantry. C. C. Winnis, former First Sergeant, was made First Lieutenant in the Eleventh Cavalry.

Noncommissioned Officers and Privates.

Allen, H. A.	Lomasney, D. F.
Arendell, A. J.	Long, John.
Arnold, A. J.	Lowe, Jas. T.
Baine, Thomas F.	Martin, W.
Baker, V.	Meadows, Thos. J.
Biddle, Earl.	Miller, J. W.
Blankinship, A. B.	Mitchell, G. J.
Brazelton, Clyde.	Morrison, F.
Brown, Jas.	Mosby, H.
Chisholm, S. S.	Moore, Don D.
Chisholm, A. J.	Morgan, J. M.
Crump, C. L.	Myers, W. E.
Dauldburn, Alexis.	O'Leary, D.
Doherty, G. W.	Price, W. J.
Dutcher, C.	Quarles, Jas. T.
Edwards, T.	Rash, G. B.
Eldridge, J. R.	Roan, R.
Ellis, P.	Reed, P.
Frizzell, O. C.	Rosser, M.
Gallipher, F.	Rowley, J. H.
Gallimore, J. I.	Rundle, J. W.
Gallimore, Wm. E.	Settle, B.
Gass, John.	Sheppard, H. N.
Gore, Luke T.	Simpson, D. P.
Graves, E. G.	Speakman, M.
Hallersley, M. J.	Stanford, Zeb.
Hayes, R. L.	Sweeney, Henry B.
Hilton, John F.	Taylor, W. P.
Heinz, E. R.	Taylor, R. L.
Huber, Elwood.	Thomas, F.
Johnson, R. D.	Tansley, Leslie.
Jolley, W. F.	Turner, G. F.
Jones, Jas. L.	Van Hoover, G. H.
Keeling, James.	Wheeler, Leroy.
Kinkead, W. W.	Whatman, M. H.
Lacey, Oscar.	Whittaker, J. A.
Lester, Evan.	Whittaker, G. F.
Linneville, J. W.	Williams, H. A.
Lu J. Jas. M.	Young, Sergio.

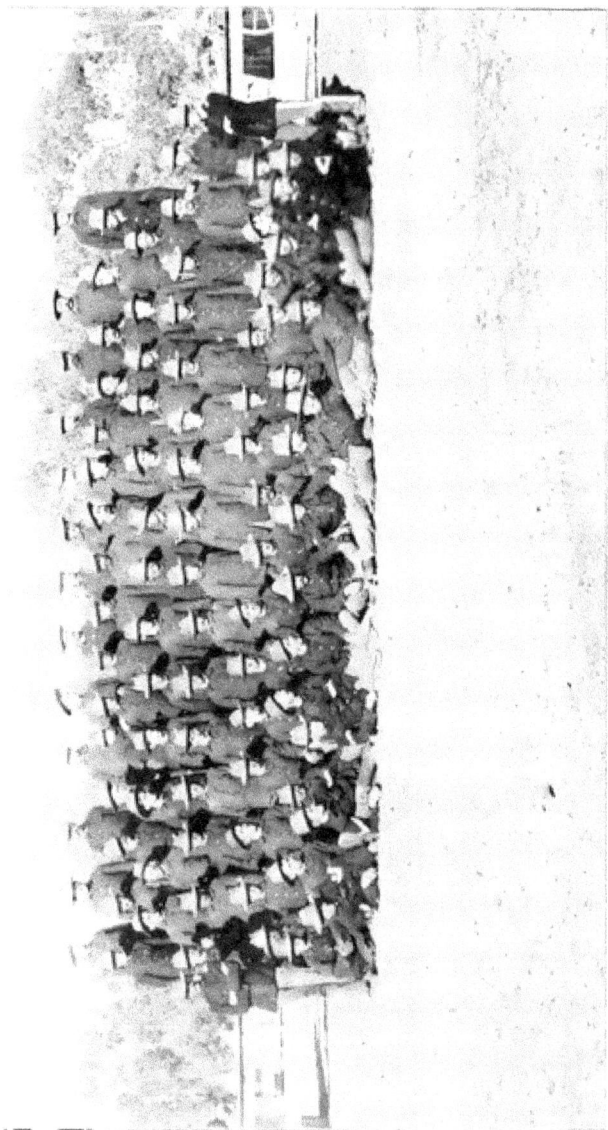

SUSPENSION BRIDGE AT MANILA.
CROSSED OFTEN BY TENNESSEANS GOING TO BILIBID PRISON

COMPANY D.

William J. Galbreath, Captain.

Edward C. McNeal, First Lieutenant.

Edson E. McNeely, Second Lieutenant.

Joe B. Cocke, former Second Lieutenant, was transferred to the Thirty-seventh Infantry. Mark G. Fakes, former Duty Sergeant, was made Quartermaster Sergeant and Second Lieutenant.

Noncommissioned Officers and Privates.

Alexander, C.
Alexander, Edward.
Alred, James W.
Anderson, Lem O.
Bidwell, G. L.
Blair, Chas. W.
Blair, Paine B.
Boyd, Geo. W.
Bradon, H. H.
Brown, Neal.
Bryant, Clay V.
Bryant, Wm. C.
Bumpass, Thos. L.
Bumpass, Willie A.
Bush, J. L.
Carter, Wm. H.
Clark, John O.
Clark, Walter C.
Cornet, George.
Cureton, Marion L.

Davis, G. W.
Downing, J. T.
Drake, G. W.
Duffin, Chas. A.
Elliott, W. R.
Gallaher, John A.
Garland, W. H.
Guthrie, Frank.
Guthrie, Will.
Hall, Joe.
Harvill, M. M.
Harvill, H. W.
Hickey, Edward.
Holt, Fred A.
Hooks, Albert L.
Horn, Lee.
Humbert Jas. H.
Jackson, Benj.
Keene, James T.
Kimber, Robt. L.

Langford, Hick.
Ledbetter, N. P.
Marshall, P. E.
Marsh, Geo. D.
McClanahan A. C.
Milam, Edward S.
Neeley, Wm.
Petty, Alex B.
Plaskett, C. G.
Porter, Allen L.
Sherrell, Wm. B.
Smith, Thos. R.
Staley, James D.
Starr, Chas. L.

Sutton, Dennis.
Troxel, George.
Troxel, Rufus.
Washburn, C. A.
Weaver, Will.
Westdahl, Ford.
White, Looney A.
Wiles, Calvin.
Wilson, Chas. W.
Winford, Hugh.
Wright, Atticus B.
Wright, Mark J.
Ziegenbein, John.

COME SEVEN! COME LEVEN!

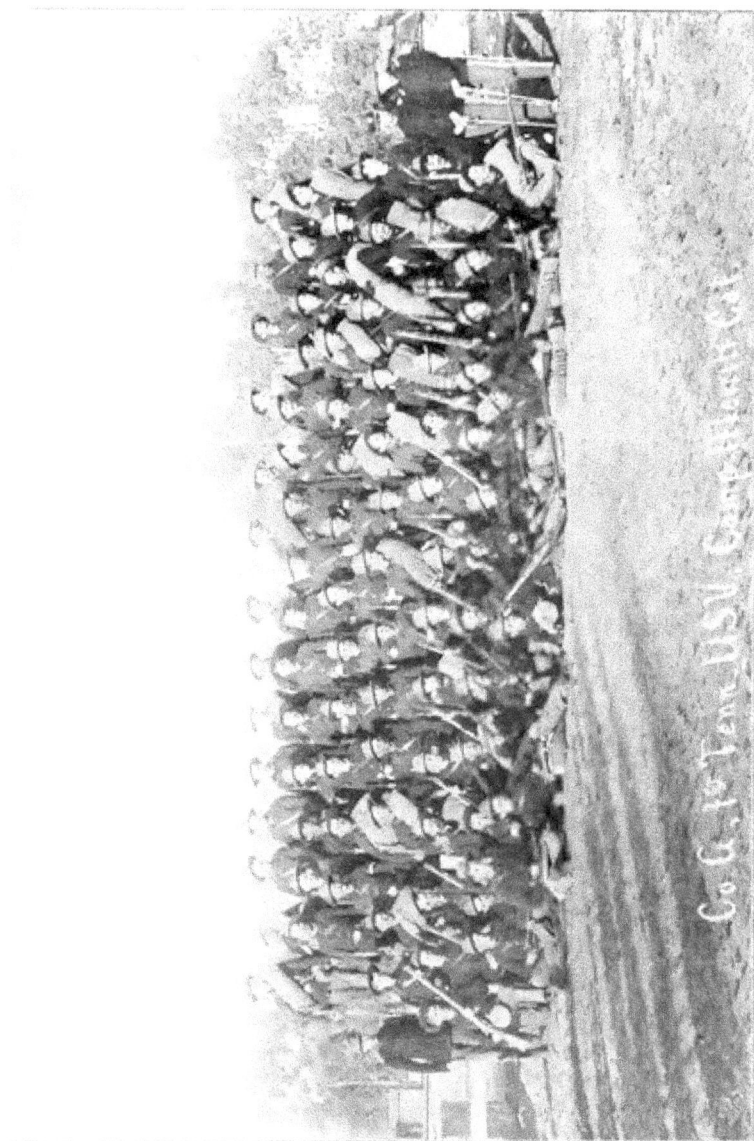

Co. C, 1st Tenn. N.S.V. Camp Hamilton, Va.

BAYONET EXERCISE, SAN FRANCISCO, CAL.

COMPANY E.

James Hager, Captain.

S. M. Williams, First Lieutenant.

Nick Malone, Second Lieutenant.

G. L. Chapman, former First Lieutenant, was transferred to the Thirty-seventh Infantry

Noncommissioned Officers and Privates.

Austin, P.
Bader, H. H.
Barfield, C. A.
Barry, J. L.
Battle, Frank.
Bigley, D. W.
Billis, O. J.
Bonner, W. G.
Bowden, Rufe.
Burton, R. H.
Buchanan, J. M.
Caskey, J. L.
Cassetty, M.
Choat, H. R.
Clemons, H. D.
Curry, J. H., Jr.
Curry, R. O.
Dillard, W. G.
Douthett, B. C.
Davis, G. W.
Davis, Albert.
Durdan, John.
Gant, Wm. P., Jr.
Godwin, J.
Greer, Frank.
Griffin, E. V.
Griffin, W. E.
Grigsby, L. K.
Gossman, C. H.
Hardiman, Frank.
Haskins, Ben.
Hester, Bert.
Hirshberg, N.
Hopkins, Thos.
Hughes, Karl.

Irving, J. T.
Johnson, T. J.
Jones, G.
Jordan, G.
King, W. W.
Kirkpatrick, J. D.
Lampley, C. F.
Lawrence, L. P.
Lee, W. T.
Love, J. R.
Malone, Geo. S.
McCroskey, E. J.
McFarland, C. A.
McGinnis, J.
Moore, R. L.
Moore, J. B.
Morrison, W. L.
Morton, Bob.
O'Connor, R. L.
Pool, F. B.
Rains, L. A.
Robinson, D. A.
Rose, G. P.
Ross, E. A.
Scott, C. E.
Searle, B. E.
Shelton, L. J.
Shelton, J. R.
Wade, Jos. L.
Weimer, A. H.
West, J. E.
Williams, E. W.
Williamson, E. B.
Woolard, C. F.

COMPANY F.

James Knox Polk, Captain.

H. H. Eastman, First Lieutenant.

Thomas E. Halbert, Second Lieutenant.

A. C. Gillem, former Captain, made Major of the regiment. R. M. Milam, former First Lieutenant, made Captain Company B.

Noncommissioned Officers and Privates.

Allmond, S. E.
Anderson, R. N.
Arnett, C. F.
Ballentine, O. V.
Barry, R. P.
Black, N. P.
Branch, W. F.
Brown, Leon.
Brown, J. E.
Carter, J. W.
Denton, Wm.
Duff, J. H.
Fertig, T. P.
Fessler, Z.
Freeman, C. E.
Gaines, J. M.
Green, Dock.
Griffin, N. K.
Grimes, E. L.
Guthrie, L. K.
Hampel, T. N.
Handley, E. M.
Hills, O. G.
Hillman, L. W.
Hills, F. H.
Holbrooth, J. M.
Humphreys, Geo.
Haven, W. H.
Lusk, C. F.
Jenkins, J. C.

Knapp, C. W.
Malone, J. W.
Mangrum, W. N.
Mayes, G. W.
McCarthy, H. C.
McDaniel, F.
Milam, J. H.
Nunnally, E. M.
Partin, M. A.
Phillips, S. N.
Prater, G. H.
Regen, J. H.
Richardson, D. L.
Schlotter, C. H.
Short, P. H.
Slabey, C. E.
Smallwood, W. S.
Smoot, J. H.
Stone, D. S.
Surgonat, J. G.
Savage, E. A.
Tanner, A. W.
Taylor, E. C.
Thompson, J. N.
Turner, W. G.
Vick, L. S.
Walsh, E. L.
Waters, W. T.
Winslow, B. P.
Warren, R. B.

1 LIEUT. C. M. McLESTER.
2 LIEUT. T. E. HALBERT.
3 LIEUT. CAVE JOHNSON
4 LIEUT. C. A. RICHARDSON
5 LIEUT. JAMES W. MOORE.
6 LIEUT. H. H. EASTMAN

AN INNOCENT PASTIME.

COMPANY G.

Hugh Sparkman, Captain.

Thomas F. Bates, First Lieutenant.

Frank Blakemore, Second Lieutenant.

H. B. Myers, former Captain, was transferred to the Thirty-seventh Infantry. J. W. Moore, former Duty Sergeant, was made Second Lieutenant of Company I.

Noncommissioned Officers and Privates.

Auchinbaugh, J.	McClendon, M. B.
Bigley, C. S.	McDermott, J.
Blacknall, A.	Mercer, Will.
Blanton, L. W.	Mitchell, Will.
Brannan, W. C.	Moore, Chas.
Brown, Joe.	Myers, Claude.
Creasey, Felix.	Neal, Jas.
Creasey, J. P.	Odum, J. P.
Creasey, Munroe.	Peters, A. V.
Daniels, M. P.	Phillips, M. G.
Davis, B. P.	Powell, J. H.
Davis, John.	Puterbaugh, C. P.
Deal, D. W.	Quillen, D. P.
Durham, J. W.	Ray, J. H.
Dyer, J. E.	Rector, H. W.
Ferrell, J. A.	Redden, J. T.
Gartner, Henry.	Redman, S. O.
Green, A. J.	Reynolds, R. P.
Gross, Geo.	Robinson, R.
Hancock, J. H.	Rozzell, Ed.
Harrison, Dock.	Slatton, W. A.
Harrison, O. C.	Sloan, J. W.
Hudson, T. R.	Speck, D. A
Huffaker, Emial.	Suddeth, O. R.
Jackson, J. H	Tresp, Will.
Jessup, Leonard.	Weir, A. P.
Jones, J. A.	Wherton, J. L.
Knight, C. S.	Whittaker, M. H.
Mahaffey, Wm.	Williams, J. G.
Martin, J. W.	Willingham, L. W.
McClain, A. R.	

COMPANY H.

Gaston O'Brien, Captain.

Bowman Ewing, First Lieutenant.

J. Willis Burks, Second Lieutenant.

Cave Johnson, former First Lieutenant, and Patrick L. Stacker, former Second Lieutenant, discharged.

Noncommissioned Officers and Privates.

Atkinson, John G.	Miles, Robert.
Bradley, Wm.	Moody, J. S.
Bramer, James.	Moran, Wm. T.
Brown, C. L.	Morenold, Wm.
Buckingham, T. E.	Morrow, W. H.
Burton, Patrick.	Morrow, Nick.
Clenn, Ernest.	Owens, L. D.
Clifton, Samuel.	Perkins B. R.
Collbain, B. N.	Prater, Edward.
Cooke, H. T.	Pulley, John.
Daniel, H. L.	Ralls, C. C.
Driscoll, Richard.	Randle, Underwood.
Eldridge, Wm.	Roberts, J. P.
Ewing, Bowman.	Rosenfield, C.
Forbes, Wm. A.	Sargent, W. O.
Foster, E. J.	Sands, John M.
Gray, E. E.	Sheppard, J. A
Harrison, A. B.	Sheepman, J. W.
Heggie, Leon A.	Smith, V. H.
Hoskins, Wm.	Sullivan, D. H.
Hunter, John.	Taylor, D. L.
Hyman, Edward.	Tidwell, C. C.
Jacks, A. E.	Triplett, R. K.
Jackson, Perry.	Tuck, P. W.
Johnson, Boyd.	Weaks, C. E.
Ligon, G. W.	White, C. H.
Lowry, P. M.	Williams, W. H.
Mason, C. J.	Woodhead, L. F.
McAllister, Kay.	Wright, Chas.
Mellon, N.	

OVER THE WASHTUB

1. LIEUT. PATRICK STACKER
2. LIEUT. N. N. PICKARD
3. LIEUT. NICK MALONE
4. LIEUT. BOWMAN EWING
5. LIEUT. MORGAN WILLIAMS
6. LIEUT. WINSTON PILCHER

SERGT. CLEMENT C. JONES.
WHO CAPTURED A FILIPINO FLAG

COMPANY I.

Leon Caraway, Captain.

Ernest Bowles, First Lieutenant.

J. W. Moore, Second Lieutenant.

Nick N. Givens, former Captain, was transferred to the Thirty-seventh Infantry.

Noncommissioned Officers and Privates.

Alexander, J. W.	Eddings, Jesse.
Beaton, Will L.	Fair, Henry.
Bottsford, Louis I.	Gillтом, O. H.
Boyett, Wm. R.	Glass, Dan.
Bannan, E.	Glover, R. E.
Bowser, W. T.	Hall, Robert.
Butcher, Thos. W.	Hatfield, A. L.
Carnan, R. S.	Hess, John.
Chambers, J. L.	Howard, Jesse.
Chittwood, Richard.	Hughes, T. C.
Chittwood, Ed.	Jeffries, John.
Clarey, Wm.	Jeffries, LeRoy.
Crosswhite, M.	Jeffries, Pleas.
Curd, Richard.	Jeffries, Silas.
Davis, J. M.	Johnson, Joe.
Douglas, L. G.	Looper, C. W.
Dowdy, Jesse A.	Maden, Silas.

Maupin, W. C.	Reed, Balem.
McCortt, J. R.	Rexsden, Isaac.
McGee, G. W.	Robbins, W. R.
McDonald, B.	Sanders, M.
Nelson, Ed.	Sellars, Bruce.
Oliver, John P.	Sexton, J. M.
Peters, R. K.	Sexton, Marion.
Petitit, Ross.	Sloan, Ben F.
Phillips, B. O.	Stansbury, Will.
Phillips, Thomas.	Waters, James.
Phillips, Thos. L.	West, J. M.
Reed, A. J.	Zillner, C. F.

COMPANY K.

Samuel O. Murphey, Captain.

Nixon N. Pickard, First Lieutenant.

Charles A. Richardson, Second Lieutenant.

John C. Patton, former First Lieutenant, was transferred to the Thirty-seventh Infantry.

Noncommissioned Officers and Privates.

Beasley, A. N.	Murray, J. W.
Bolinger, Ed N.	Myatt, John.
Briley, Chas.	Officer, John.
Brown, Robt.	Patterson, J. R.
Burke, Gordon L.	Peters, J. B.
Byrd, Thos. R.	Peters, R. H.
Cotton, L. M.	Phillips, John W.
Crosby, H. A.	Pinkerton, R. Lee.
Crawford, Robt.	Plummer, F. S.
Cudworth, Edward.	Plummer, Thos. M.
Barrow, Frank B.	Richardson, Robert I.
Ferguson, E. A.	Ross, Matthew.
Fizer, Joe.	Rosson, John B.
Fly, Wm.	Sheldon, G. R.
Frazier, Guy.	Smith, F. A.
Freeman, Allen M.	Smith, W. C.
Geer, Tim.	Smith, Sam G.
Gray, R. H.	Talley, J. N.
Harris, W. H.	Thomas, J. L.
Hendricks, T. W.	Tingley, J. E.
Honeycutt, R. B.	Walker, Frank.
Huggins, L. H.	Ward, Rufus.
Johnson, T. B.	Warren, Alexander.
Jones, J. G.	Warren, M. R.
Kelly, Hopkins.	Webb, Waits.
Loton, John.	White, G. J.
Luton, Robt.	Whitney, C. V.
McCabe, John.	Wilhoite, Tom.
Merrifield, C. P.	Windes, M. O.
Morrison, C. W.	Wright, F. G.
Morris, Ed.	

1. CAPT. TOM ELLIS.
2. ARTHUR S. EWING.
3. LIEUT. A. W. CABLER.
4. CAPT. LOGAN WILLIAMS.
5. QUAR. M. C. CAMPBELL.
6. LONNIE POLK.

COMPANY L.

Carles C. Van Leer, Captain.
William Caruthers, First Lieutenant.
W. P. Cooper, Second Lieutenant.

Sem Van Leer, former Captain, was transferred to the Thirty-seventh Infantry. Winston Pilcher, former Second Lieutenant, was made First Lieutenant Company H, afterwards transferred to the Thirty-seventh Infantry. Nat Gooch, former private, was made Second Lieutenant Company M.

Noncommissioned Officers and Privates.

Anderson, Chas. B.	Cook, M.
Baker, J. E.	Coop, W. W.
Bayless, W. P.	Crockett, D. T.
Berry, Chas.	Corkett, H. Y.
Bowman, F. M.	Crocker, E.
Bratton, W. G.	Is Ben, W.
Burke, M.	Davis, Wm.
Childress, S. C.	Cook, S. T. C.

Fowler, G.		Maynor, W. E.
Felton, Ira.		Melton, W. C.
Fromt, G. W.		Nichol, Geo. E.
Galloway, M.		Oliver, E. R.
Grimsley, W. L.		Parker, Harry
Hannah, S. M.		Phillips, E. B.
Hard, Wm.		Ridley, Eugene
Hare, C. A.		Robinson, B. D.
Hillman, C. E.		Sivoli, Tony
House, R. L.		Sloan, W. B.
Hynes, D. P.		Smiley, W. S.
Jenkins, E.		Stratford, J.
Jones, B. C.		Suddath, A. G.
Kinney, W. P.		Suddath, W. S.
Knox, Frank T.		Tierney, Jas.
Large, D. P.		Turner, P. T.
Lesson, John		Whitson, R. R.
Leathers, G. W.		Wood, S. L.
Lennerly, W. T.		Wood, T. F.
Leslie, A. T.		Workman, C. E.
Lovell, R. L.		

BAYONET EXERCISE, SAN FRANCISCO, CAL.

COMPANY M.

Sheffield Clark, Captain.
Martin Bismukes, First Lieutenant.
Nat Gooch, Second Lieutenant.

Noncommissioned Officers and Privates.

Archibald, W. A.	Cowan, John.
Baggett, A.	Critz, T. L.
Bass, G. R.	Ewang r, W. F.
Brunford, F. P.	Fewell, J. P.
Benzeck, G. H.	Fox, J. E.
Byrns, J. M.	Green, s. J. F.
Blair, S. F.	Freeman, R.
Bratton, S. C.	French, Bristol
Chrisman, J. M.	Hagler, Lewis
Cleveland, G. W.	Harris, E. A.
Cook, Fred	Hedly, T. J.
Capdell, G. N.	Heximer, Chas. H.

Hickey, H. B.	Ridner, Ross
Hoppes, C. A.	Riggie, T. L.
Hosea, J. H.	Riley, W. A.
Huches, G. W.	Rodgers, N. F.
Jacobson, J. S.	Rutledge, a. H.
Jones, J. N.	Saunders, E. O.
Jones, B. N.	Sawyers, J. J.
Knopke, W. F.	Settle, J. P.
Ledbetter, Frank	Scott, W. L.
Little, W. R.	Stout, G. B.
Mackel, J. J.	Stuck, L. L.
McPerra, W. N.	Sullivan, n. H.
Miller, F. R.	Tiller, G. E.
Nesl, Nat	Weldon, Ed.
Nelson, C. A.	Wells, J.
Newsom, J. B.	Whitehead, T. B.
Pope, Geo.	Wixson, C. A.
Porter, R. K.	Young, A. H.
Prince, William	

1. GEN. MILLER REVIEWING TROOPS.   2. DRESS PARADE.   3. BATTALION DRILL.

COL. W. C. SMITH AND STAFF.

DISCHARGED AT MANILA

IN THIS LIST THE GREATER PART RE-ENLISTED, AND A NUMBER LEFT THE PHILIPPINES FOR A TRIP AROUND THE WORLD. A FEW CAME ON TO SAN FRANCISCO.

COMPANY A.

Averill, F. L.
Ball, V. L.
Beatty, J. E.
Beresford, C. H.
Buckner, C.
Cabrut, J. N
Crutchfield, E.
Duckworth, J. T.
Fitzpatrick, J. E.
Fitzpatrick, K.
Grizzard, H. D.
Howery, J.
Hodge, J. H.

Kimball, A. L.
Martindale, M. J.
Mix, Harry.
Newkirk, A. J.
Peck, R. H.
Prann, M. B.
Pierce Maurice J.
Roberts, E.
Smith, C. M.
Stewart, F.
Todd, C. S.
Wharton, J. H.

Hart, R. E.
Jackson, Wm.
Lockhart, N. H.
McKissack, R. L.
Morgan, J. H.
Notgrass, C. B.
Ormes, L. B.
Overton, W. J.
Payne, Claude.
Price, J. C.
Ray, Lovick.
Reed, W. L.

Russell, P. F.
Simpson, L. O.
Skillern, R. C.
Slaight, J. T.
Smythe, J. M.
Solinsky, H.
Spurlin, Gains.
Spencer, J. B.
Strong, L. P.
Watts, W. O.
Watts, H. C.
Wright, F. D.

COMPANY B.

Batts, T. N.
Berry, C. R., Jr.
Bruges, H. E.
Burns, Chas.
Cook, R. R.

Cowden, J. W.
Crane, L.
Dodson, Edward.
Grimes, J. L.
Glenn, W. H.

COMPANY C.

Allison, W. F.
Birdwell, Jas. K.
Daniels, J. H.
Ellis, Luke.
Gatinbie, L.
Hall, P. M.
Hicks, Jeff.

Jermain Jas.
Jones, Grant.
Martin, D. R.
Nine Alonzo.
Steakley, D. L.
Tothacer, Jas. M.
Williams, B.

1 CAPT JAS K POLK.
2 CAPT A J LAW.

3 CAPT SAM VAN LEER.
4 CAPT R M MILAM.
5 CAPT HU B MYERS

6. CAPT L A CARAWAY
7. CAPT GEORGE REED.

LIEUT. W. F. COOPER.

COMPANY F.

Alexander, James	Clase, D. L.
Beaumont, H. E.	Huggans, L. R.
Bruce, Wm. R.	Nelly, C. J.
Carpishell, A. M.	Kinzer, N. J.
Carson, O. H.	Mann, W. S.
Chapman, F. E.	Mickle, J. M.
Collingsworth, B. F.	Rea, R. M.
Fleming, F. H.	Roberts, F. O.
Gibbs, Q. D.	Rutter, Wm.
Gillem, S. J.	Sammels, J. H.
Gillespie, J. W.	Sammels, O. W.
Gillock, R. F.	Sawyer, L. E.

COMPANY G.

Alexander, J. S.	Knowles, J. G.
Barrett, A. M.	Little, Thos. L.
Bell, Monson	Moore, J. W.
Brothers, H. R.	Osborne, W. T.
Connor, E. B.	Stephens, Henry.
Finney, J. I.	Tucker, W. H.
Floyd, Geo.	Wallace, C. C.
Glasgow, J. T.	Wailer, J. W.
Haggerty, P. P.	White, Horace
Henderson, John	Williams, J. W.
Holder, C. A.	Wood, J. H.
Jones, T.	Wright, R. E.
Johnson, Will	

COMPANY D.

Armstrong, W. F.	Oleson, Ole J.
Barker, John	Owen, Basil
Bloom, Calvin H.	Pennington, C. W.
Brothers, C. L.	Plaskett, J. W.
Brooks, Cos. C.	Potts, Sam T.
Coffman, John	Richard, Clarence
Costner, Wm. R.	Saddler, P. E.
Crownover, J. M.	Stanford, Walter
Drake, Mark P.	Strong, L. R.
Inman, S. E.	Vollas, James
Kelly, W. J.	Wallace, Milton E.
McNeal, Chester G.	Wildes, Calvin
Moore, Milton M.	

COMPANY E.

Battle, George	Lee, Harry
Browder, W. C.	La, J. E.
Crandall, T. A.	McCord, N. L.
Delong, Thos	Pool, L. C.
Doyle, John	Rooker, C. A.
Pryor, R. H.	Ryan, Chas.
Pulley, Felix	Sirtis, R. A.
Gibson, A. V.	Thompson, W. L.
Johnson, James	Vickers, E.
Johnson, O. W.	Watson, Clyde

WAITING MARCHING ORDERS.

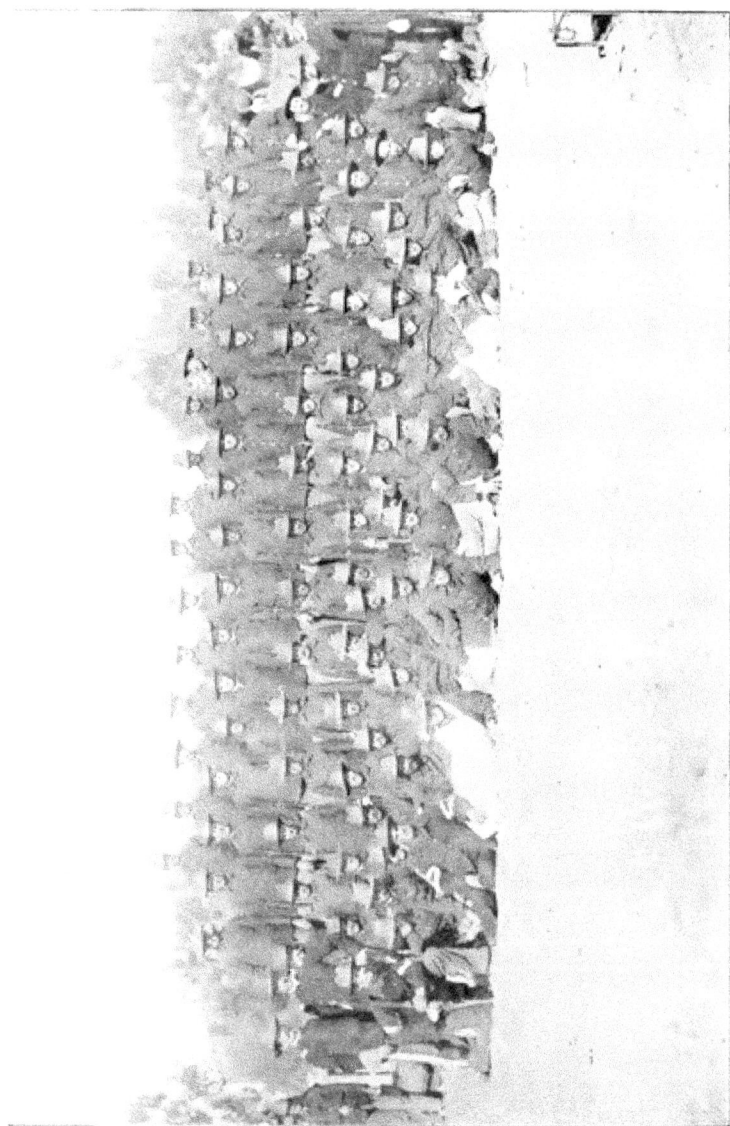

REVIEW AT THE PRESIDIO TENNESSEE REGIMENT PASSING GENERAL MILLER

COMPANY H.

Curtis, J.
Davidson, W. E.
Dorris, L. C.
Drane, Lewis
Eaker, Chas.
Ellis, Thos. H.
Evans, A. O.
Hudson, M. J.
Kendrick, J. C., Jr.
Lambrecht, H.
Mabry, Thos.

McCleary, Edward.
Miller, W.
Moore, C. L.
Poore, J. Z.
Rollow, E. W.
Smith, R. B.
Stacker, Clay, Jr.
Stewart, S.
Tate, John H.
Williamson, Logan.
Woodhead, H. F.

COMPANY I.

Alexander, W. T.
Alton, Wm. H.
Carriger, G. C.
Coulter, Richard.
Duff, J. T.
Dye, Chas. B.
Ensory, Alex.
Geer, Geo.
George, Lee.
Leach, D. F.
Litton, Harvey.
Llewellyn, Jas.
Long, John W.

Martin, W. H.
McGinnis, W. P.
McFadden, W. A.
Moore, Walter.
Moses, Jas. H.
Munpower, Sam.
Newport, M.
Orange, N. P.
Phillips, Josiah.
Redman, J. A.
Scott, Frean.
Taylor, J. W.
Taylor, Sherman.

COMPANY K.

Butler, A. J.
Crossland, Edward.
Davis, Edward.
Davidson, W. M.
Dufer, J. F.
Fathers, J. E.
Fox, John P.

Garrett, Andrew.
Hardacre, C. G.
Hart, J. H.
Hodge, R. M.
Jones, S. B.
Meros, W. S.
Myatt, T. Lee.

COMPANY L.

Askew, R.
Bass, R. J.
Bowling, W. K.
Clark, J. C.
Coslett, J. R.
Cummins, J. D.
David, C. R.
Fletcher, J. L.
Gooch, Nat.
Grandall, Jas.
Graves, G. L.
Green, J. G.
Johnson, L. E.
Jones, J. R.
Jones, W. G.

Lavelle, James.
Lucas, J. D.
Maunon, W.
McEwen, John A., Jr.
Morris, Robt.
Morton, W. P.
Nichols, J.
Nichols, L.
Smith, C. P.
Smith, T. W.
Snyder, J. R.
Walker, R. H.
Walker, W. J.
White, Wm.

COMPANY M.

Allen, G. L.
Burgett, John.
Curley, R. W.
Davis, R. E.
Foster, T. P.
Esvall, H. E.
Hudson, N. J.
Griffith, R.
Hicks, R. C.
Litchfield, L. O.

Powers, Chas.
Proctor, Wm. J.
Reed, Robert
Rodgers, R. L.
Roth, Emile.
Smalling, John.
Tandy, Jesup S.
Taylor, Benjamin.
Thornburg, John P.
Tabler, J. S.
Watkins, S. D.

Preston, W. R.
Smith, Andrew.
Smith, F. B.
Stokes, Ed.
Strunk, J. M.
Sullivan, T. E.
Talbot, Jos.
Talley, Otto.
Taylor, J. T.
Tudor, J. R.

1. OFF FOR MANILA.   2. THE TRANSPORT INDIANA RETURNING TO AMERICA.

Others Discharged.

In addition to those named above as having been discharged in the Philippines, the following, whose names cannot be found in the regimental roster, are given:

Noncommissioned Staff—W. R. Davis, Boyd Johnson, Arthur E. Emory, Frank A. Smith, George J. Smith.

Band—L. C. Gaylord, Frank A. Wright.

Company A—Jas. T. Bremming, Chas. P. Thruston, C. Walter Gowan.

Company B—P. C. Seymour, Lee K. Pona, E. Alexander.

Company E—Ed Gregory, L. P. Woodley, J. P. Davidson, O. J. Kirkland.

Company I—W. T. James.

Company L—J. E. Brown, Joseph Fletcher, C. B. Ewing, Charles Richardson.

Company H—J. M. Rander.

Company G—C. B. Montgomery, James D. Moss, Emile Bertner, Roy Johnson, F. Blakemore, E. Powell.

Company F—A. F. Grimes, J. F. Knapp, Chas. Leonard.

Company C—C. C. Winn.

Company M—T. L. Richards, J. Ford, E. O. Samuels, D. H. Sibbett, John Plaskett.

Company K—Harry Johnson, R. H. McDonald, G. R. Duffin, John K. Zilgenheim, Wm. A. Garland, Hopkins K. Ellick.

Those who determined to make a trip around the world were:

R. S. Coulter.   R. C. Crutchfield.
C. H. Stacker.   M. Martindale.
E. W. Rollow.   M. J. Pierce.
Boyd Johnson.   C. L. Baker.
J. N. Rundle.   J. H. Tate.
Y. C. Kendrick.   J. N. Wharton.

Logan Williamson and H. L. Frierson went to Europe via the Suez Canal.

Percy L. Jones, Captain and Assistant Surgeon, and K. M. Kirby-Smith, Captain and Assistant Surgeon, remained in the Philippines to practice medicine.

Discharged in 1898.

Following is the list of soldiers discharged at San Francisco, in October, 1898.

Band—Privates Hope, Baker, Lewis, Floyd, and W. Hugh Harris.

Company A—Privates Luther L. Banks, Thomas Goodall, John H. Grey, Thomas Nixon, Nathan P. Harris, Patrick H. Russell, Carl F. Shoffner, Harry L. Scott, Fred L. Stewart, Karl Stokes, Harry Winn, A. L. Windle, R. W. and Thomas Woods.

Company B—Sergt. Robert R. Compton, Privates Israel W. Bennett, Joseph A. Bowling, John Schapman, Lemuel Cooke, Charles Good, Nat C. Hickey, William Irwin, James H. Jenkins, James S. Jenkins, Ernest Kidwell, Robt. M. Lindsley, Walter W. Marshall, Charles Metcalfe, William Newton, Harvey A. Pilkington, T. Albert Redley, Honey L. Smith, Rufus Stokes, Martin Taylor, Daniel Ware.

Company C—Privates William H. Birdwell, James Cook, Frank Fitzgerald, William E. Harris, Luther Kirkpatrick, Henry Longworth, Joseph Smith, William W. Robinson.

Company D—Privates Reuben J. Brown, Ambrose Burger, William E. Cary, John B. Free, Felix R. Gibson, Henry Jones, Nelson Llewellyn, William Moffatt, Russell M. Sharp, Edgar B. Washburn, Morgan R. Wonaman.

Company E—Privates Adam Diehl, Jr., P. H. Parish, J. W. Moore, Wm. R. Jenkins, R. M. Saunders, Jr., Fred J. Sitzler, James S. Cincunago.

Company F—Privates Marion C. Beaty, Charles Bonville, Hal Ledford, Alexander R. McCorkle, Charles T. Neal, James S. Parker, Felix Smith, Raphael S. Wright.

Company G—Corporals J. F. Manning and Ab Sims, Privates Lee Able, Marion J. Barnett, H. Clay Craig, John F. Gibson, John Q. Lewis, Thos. B. Masson, Walter McBride, Carl B. Montgomery, Lawrence B. Sanford, Alexander Sheppard, Thomas J. Smart, Smith Stewart, Austin Talley, Robert C. Worsham, J. Ewing Wright.

Company H—Corporal Howard Bland, and Privates James H. Adkits, George H. Benson, Jackson Beymer, Walter Chester, James Claypool, William P. Ewell, Richard V. Gossett, Joseph Gunter, Charles Hanatty, Walton Hurst, John W. Jackson, Albert G. Jenkins, Horace G. Saunderson, Alexander Sheppard, Gus Summer, John H. Williams, George W. Waller.

Company I—Privates Perry Byrd, James L. Collins, Charles F. Hoard, Albert W. Lame, George W. Lame, Jesse D. Lewis, James L. Lovelace, John Muscovalley, Millard F. Newport, John S. Robertson, Porter Sellars, Gilbert Sexton, William Z. Sharp, Eugine Travis, Paul G. White, Gaines Whitecotton.

Company K—Privates Albert E. Cadworth, William W. Cox, John Deen, Edward H. England, Henry Ferguson, Lawson C. Gunn, Mann G. Gunn, Thomas W. Gunn, William H. Halsey, Frank W. Leyley, Lawrence B. Nichols, and Walter Walling.

Company L—Sergt. Gideon Fields, Corporals John R. Aylor, William M. Petty, and Thomas P. Poe, Privates William L. Bailey, Edward J. Dougherty, John H. Douglass, James M. Douglass, George Duncan, William F. Gourley, Horace McGee, William H. McVay, Robt. L. McKinney, Edward L. Moss, George Phillips, Charles Post, Eugene Whitson.

Company M—Sergt. John H. Bright, Corporal Chas. A. Clegg, Privates L. Graton Bright, Hugh E. Bligh, William F. Cox, John B. Collins, Little B. Cotton, T. Fred Cook, Milton B. Davidson, Ready Dokohn, George K. Edward, George K. Fletcher, Martin L. Holt, James W. McClanahan, John McKinney, Jos. C. McNett, Richard Miles, Christopher Nielson, Flim Smith-Hand, Robert L. Tosh, Daniel C. Vaugh, John S. Wesley, and Lillicoat Waitte.

AT THE PRESIDIO, SAN FRANCISCO, CAL.

The Dead

Died

John S. Luttrell,
Private, Company [illegible], Nashville, May 21, 1898.

Luther Cates,
Private, Company G, Nashville, June 10, 1898.

John Hamilton,
Private, Company D, San Francisco, July 20, 1898.

William W. King,
Private, Company I, San Francisco, July 8, 1898.

Charles D. Gamble,
Private, Company A, San Francisco, [illegible] 1898.

Charles A. Kanady,
Private, Company E, San Francisco, July 17, 1898.

Zeb Stafford,
Private, Company C, San Francisco, July 18, 1898.

James E. Stafford,
Private, Company C, San Francisco, July 21, 1898.

Joseph L. Baker,
Private, Company B, San Francisco, July 22, 1898.

Sheldon Irving,
Private, Company E, San Francisco, July 29, 1898.

Percy B. Whittaker,
Private, Company K, San Francisco, August 12, 1898.

James Mitchell,
Private, Company [illegible], San Francisco, [illegible]

William A. Bempass,
Private, Company [illegible], San Francisco, [illegible]

Claude Payne,
Private, Company B.

Benjamin McConnell,
Private, Company E, [illegible] 1898.

Neal Mathews,
Private, Company M, San Francisco, [illegible] 1898.

A. B. McCain,
Private, Company G, Manila, [illegible] 1898.

John A. Meeks,
Private, Company H, Manila, [illegible] 1899.

William C. Smith,
[illegible] Manila, [illegible] February [illegible] 1899.

James A. Garvey,
Private, Company G, Manila, February [illegible] 1899.

Lewis J. Leland,
Chaplain, [illegible] Island of Panay, February 16, 1899.

James V. Morris,
Private, Company M, [illegible] February 18, 1899.

Fred J. Stozier,
Private, Company I, [illegible] March 12, 1899.

Joseph L. Walker,
Private, Company B, Manila, March 17, 1899.

William H. Wallace,
Private, Company I, Manila, March 26, 1899.

Orville Mercer,
Private, Company [illegible]

William Cleeman,
[illegible]

Frank L. McNeal,
Private, Company D, San Francisco, [illegible] 1899.

Killed

Walter M. Parrish,
Private, Company C, [illegible] Iloilo, May [illegible] 1899.

Lucien B. Price,
Corporal, Company [illegible], September [illegible] 1899.

James C. Bullington,
Corporal, Company E, [illegible] Iloilo, [illegible]

A FILIPINO BEAUTY

"OUR BOYS."

(THE FIRST TENNESSEE REGIMENT.)

In amongst the city's bustle, out amongst the rural ways,
These, "our boys," passed on unnoticed, in the uneventful days.
Peace held sway and, all untroubled, half forgot that war's alarm
Might yet roar about her pathway with the voices of the storm.

But there came a day when insult was accorded to the flag;
As the tocsin rang out shrilly, who would recreant prove or lag?
True there hovered in the distance prospects of a direful fate
But our hero-sons responded, fearless, stalwart, and elate!

Let us render them the homage that the regiment earned well
Through the nights of anxious waiting, through the days of shot and
    shell.
Liberty is not in danger whatsoever threat annoys,
Long as she can have such champions as she has to-day, "our boys!"

1 WAITING THE TRAIN FOR SAN FRANCISCO.   2 AT CHEROKEE PARK, NEAR NASHVILLE JUNE 10 1898

COMMITTEES

GENERAL COMMITTEE ON ARRANGEMENTS AND RECEPTION.

M. T. Bryan, Chairman; R. V. H. Rey, Secretary; John Allison, Tully Brown, S. A. Champion, G. H. Baskette, John D. Anderson, E. C. Lewis, Patton Cheatham, Will Cummins, M. F. Cockrill, Jos. Warner, Dr. John A. Curry, Lytton Taylor, L. B. Eastman, Andrew Milam, Dr. Nat Gooch, Dr. R. R. Fort, Capt. George Hagar, Capt. W. R. Garrett, Capt. West Morton, M. B. Pilcher, Wm. Stewart, Oliver Timothy, James L. Demoville, George S. Kinney, Theo. Cooley, Rev. Ira Landrith, Rev. J. J. Vance, C. S. Caldwell, W. L. Dudley, A. D. Wharton, W. K. Phillips, John Hitchcock, Jacob Geiger, John Caruthers, John H. Polk, James Crutchfield, Thomas Goodall, B. J. McCarthy, H. W. Buttorff, Jos. R. West, Rev. Isadore Lewinthal, Rev. Dr. Ellis, Capt. Hutcheson, John C. Brown, Capt. Kramer, Jordan Stokes, R. L. Morris, C. A. Shararberger, James S. Glenn, Firman Smith, W. G. Sadler, John P. Hickman, Prof. John L. Wright, Dr. Black, John C. Ferriss, Prof. W. C. Fulvington, W. A. Cheatham, A. V. S. Lindsley, Jas. Trimble, Gen. G. P. Thruston, J. W. Bonner, John W. Childress, J. M. Anderson, Dr. J. W. Maddin, Jr., Gen. H. C. Lamb, Capt. A. J. Harris, Dr. R. A. Halley, John H. DeWitt, C. C. Trabue, Gen. W. H. Jackson, Dr. Charles Johnson, T. P. Calhoun, Dr. R. Stonestreet, Chief Henry Curran, Percy Kinnaird, L. B. Fite, A. V. Goodpasture, Dr. W. J. Morrison, Capt. b. J. Cheny, C. R. Richardson, John W. Hunter, Jos. S. Carels, A. W. Wills, Dr. D. F. Banks, Tim Johnson, Will R. Myers, O. C. Cunningham, Dr. D. B. Price, John M. Sperry, Gen. Charles Sykes, C. L. Ridley, J. M. Gaines, Henry Tanksley, H. J. Hodge, W. T. Osborne, Maj. Jo Vaulx, Baxter Smith, Nathan Cohn, M. S. Lebeck, Samuel Berger, E. B. Allen, L. H. Gray, T. O. Morris, C. H. Sanders, J. M. S. Pettitt, W. W. Smith, J. G. Summitt, O. G. Hills, G. W. W. Sweeney, H. M. Doak, W. W. Knox, Dr. W. L. Dismukes, Jos. Lindauer, R. V. Henry, J. Matt. Williams, Dr. R. L. C. White, Wm. L. Ewing, J. Taylor Stratton, Sam Newsom, Dr. A. B. Bradford, Dr. P. D. Compton, Dr. John B. Talbot, James Grundy, H. M. Meeks, Wm. Gerst, George A. Weber, J. W. Baker, Tip Gamble, Adam Diehl, George W. Fall, Gifford

Dudley, Ryan Polk, Henry Morton, J. L. McWhirter, J. H. McPhail, Jesse W. Thomas, Dr. Marvin McFerran, W. N. Willis, George McWhirter, B. H. Beazley, C. R. C. Wheeling, R. F. Moore, James Ryan, George H. Moore, Sr., Edwin A. Price, Dr. Thomas R. Newman, W. W. Page, Dr. W. T. Harwell, Wyman Reed, R. B. Buckner, Robert Curry, Charles Eastman, Jr., Dr. W. H. Halford, Pat Griffin, W. T. Hardisson, W. J. Varley, W. D. Miller, J. E. O'Bryan, Gov. Benton, Mrs. Mifflin.

Mesdames H. R. Buckner, Jas. K. Polk, C. E. Hoss, A. C. Gillem, Nat Gooch, John J. Vertrees, R. C. Beaumont, M. S. Cockrill, G. P. Ross, W. H. Bumpass, M. B. Pilcher, W. G. Sadler, J. W. Allen, Elmer Bruce, Dr. R. Dorris, R. G. Throne, John H. Baskette, J. M. Head, John C. Gaut, John M. Gaut, John W. Childress, J. S. Pilcher, L. R. Campbell, H. Solinsky, M. S. Lebeck, John W. McAlister, A. M. Shook, W. J. Morrison, Mary F. McGuire, G. W. Gifford, E. C. Andrews, Wm. Hume, J. K. Rains, Alice Ridley, W. J. McMurray, Andrew Milam, Wesley Mowson, Will Mundim, A. J. Laws, S. W. Edwards, J. B. Hancock, A. H. Robinson, W. R. Black, S. A. Champion, Percy Warner, John R. Frizzell, Spencer McHenry, W. L. Granbery, Hamilton Parkes, J. H. Acklin, John H. Reeves, Clanie Street, Ed Stahlman, W. H. Mitchell, Edward McNeely, Andrew Price, Frank Hardeman, A. S. Marks, Ittie Kinney Rene, Berry Bayless, M. T. Polk, Corinne G. Eastman, Wm. Simmons, Jesse B. Norton, Fred Cummins, Irene Sloan, Alonzo Reed, Ed Cooper, Alice Branch, Dan Kinney, W. D. Haggard.

Misses Mary Demoville, Ella Brown, Medora Cheatham, Ada Morrow, Adella Sawrie, Eunice Polk, Wilola McCord, Mary Moore, May Buxton, Mary Hoss, Louise Hall, Cora Hays, May Sadler, Addie Williamson, L. Graff Wics, Louise Bransford, Alice Rains, Louise McHenry, Willie Fall, Mary Baird, Willie Fite, Estelle Shook, Zara Ruhm, Goldine McCarthy, Louise Hale, May Grantland, Cornelia Pearce, Virginia L. Briggs, Nannie Dudley Pilcher, Elsie Briggs, Mollie Calhoune, Lucy Cummins, Addie Douglas, Summer Keith, Ada Rice, Elizabeth Price, Lizzie Atchison, Mary Mitchell, Mary M. Williams, Susie Lusk, Mamie L. Pierce, Felicia Porter, Cora Hagar, Sadie Kinney, Elizabeth Clark.

CAPT. PERCY L. JONES.

EXECUTIVE COMMITTEE.

John D. Anderson, Chairman; R. A. Hatley, Secretary; E. C. Lewis, G. H. Baskette, Dr. W. L. Dudley, H. M. Brennecke, Firman Smith, W. T. Hardison, Maj. W. H. Morton, E. R. Richardson, Jo Frank, Tully Brown, Mrs. G. P. Rose, Mrs. M. T. Polk, Mrs. H. B. Buckner, Mrs. E. C. Andrews.

FINANCE COMMITTEE.

Maj. E. C. Lewis, Chairman; Maj. J. W. Thomas, E. C. Andrews, G. N. Tillman, R. M. Dudley, L. K. Hart, Dr. J. Y. Crawford, N. D. Malone, W. D. Witherspoon, Lee Brock, Jacob Geiger, G. M. Neely, Robert Carmack, Edgar Jones, James B. Carr, Joseph Frank, John Ralam, Sr., P. A. Smith, W. C. Dibrell, F. P. McWhirter, Ike Johnson, John J. McCann, William Litterer, Dr. J. B. Murrey, Andrew Price, Edwin M. Barnes, Robert L. Campbell, Jo. M. Warren, J. W. Johnson, A. W. Wills, Dr. Nat Gooch, D. J. McCarthy, John P. Hickman, W. B. Bayless, Dr. W. B. Lee, A. R. Anderson, T. O. Morris, Mrs. G. P. Rose.

COMMITTEE TO RECEIVE THE REGIMENT AT SAN FRANCISCO.

J. W. Gaines, Chairman; H. B. Buckner, B. J. McCarthy, Mrs. Robert E. Martin, P. M. Grimm, Miss Eunice Murphy, Miss Elizabeth Kirby, Mrs. Elmer L. Bruce, Mrs. J. H. Andrews, Mrs. Alvin C. Gillem, Mrs. Alice M. Branch, Miss Mary E. Warmack, Mrs. Nathaniel Gooch, Miss Mary Hill Cockrill, Mrs. H. B. Buckner, Mrs. Mary C. Dorris, George T. Halley, Mrs. L. F. Beaumont, Mrs. M. T. Polk, Mrs. James K. Polk, Charles H. Johnson, Nashville; James A. Cheatham, Miss Kathleen O'Brien, Miss Queen, Mrs. C. W. Bailey, Mrs. Clay Stacker, Mrs. C. W. Beaumont, Miss Louise Higgie, Cave Johnson, Clarksville; Mrs. Bullock, Franklin; Mr. and Mrs. J. W. Frierson, Columbia; J. S. Chandler, Hermitage; Finis Ewing, Jr., Hampton Station; Mr. and Mrs. W. M. Brandon, Dover; W. A. McGraw, Fort Henry; Robert L. Morris, Paris; Mrs. T. M. McMellin, Hopkinsville; Mrs. John G. Maguire, McMinnville.

EMPLOYMENT COMMITTEE.

E. C. Andrews, Chairman; Capt. A. J. Harris, Chas. H. Sanders, N. D. Malone, B. J. McCarthy, W. M. Cravsty, J. B. Carr, Theodore Cooley, R. A. Hatley, C. S. Caldwell, Jo B. Morgan, W. C. Collier, Will Cummins, Joseph Lindauer, A. V. Goodpasture, John B. Ransom, Paul Eldridge, Byrd Douglas, E. B. Wrenne.

Robert Lusk, W. Dudley Gale, R. P. Webb, Hugh K. Aberson, Alex Hunter, W. P. Rutland, G. W. Brandon, L. B. Fite, G. M. Neely, T. B. Dallas, Mrs. E. C. Andrews, Mrs. G. P. Rose, Mrs. Thomas Pettus, Mrs. E. E. Hoss, Mrs. J. C. Gaut, Mrs. M. B. Pilcher, Mrs. L. L. Terry, Mrs. J. K. Rains.

INVITATION COMMITTEE.

Hon. J. M. Head, Chairman; H. M. Brennecke, G. N. Tillman, E. A. Price, L. R. Eastman, J. W. Gaines, John N. Sperry, John Caruthers, A. D. Marks, A. W. Wills.

PROGRAMME COMMITTEE.

Dr. W. L. Dudley, Chairman; G. H. Baskette, Dr. R. L. C. White, S. A. Champion, J. W. Thomas, E. C. Lewis, John D. Anderson, J. M. Head, Firman Smith, John C. Brown, W. R. Garrett, Theo. Cooley, H. M. Brennecke, Mrs. M. T. Polk, Mrs. Elmer Bruce, Mrs. E. C. Andrews, J. W. Gaines, G. P. Thruston, Gov. Benton McMillin, W. T. Hardison, John Allison, W. J. Varley, Tully Brown, M. S. Cockrill, Geo. F. Hager, W. H. Morton, Capt. W. A. T. Kramer, W. H. Morton, W. D. Miller, Mrs. Mary C. Dorris, Mrs. Berry Bayless.

TRANSPORTATION COMMITTEE.

John W. Thomas, Chairman; John D. Anderson, A. W. Wills, H. M. Brennecke, John P. Hickman, M. S. Cockrill, H. W. Buttorff, E. R. Richardson, Geo. S. Kinney, John Caruthers, Percy Kinnaird, Jesse W. Thomas, Charles Sykes, Charles H. Sanders, Russell G. Bean.

MILITARY COMMITTEE.

Capt. W. R. Garrett, Chairman; Capt. Geo. F. Hager, Capt. W. H. Morton, Capt. M. B. Pilcher, Col. Baxter Smith, Capt. Joe B. O'Bryan, Capt. W. B. Walton, Col. Thos. L. Claiborne, W. H. Bosman, Gen. H. C. Lamb, Capt. W. A. T. Kramer, Col. Hutchinson, Capt. B. G. Wood.

DECORATION COMMITTEE.

H. M. Brennecke, Chairman; O. J. Timothy, Jas. I. Bonnoville, Jo Frank, R. T. Quarles, Joe Buford, C. W. Rives, Joe M. Warren, John P. Hickman, Chas. Tritchler, Mrs. John J. Vertrees, Mrs. M. B. Pilcher, Mrs. S. A. Champion, Mrs. Birie Kinney Rene, Mrs. P. L. Blum, Miss Ella Brown, Miss Medora McAlister, Miss Idelle Sawrie, Miss Mary Dibrell, Miss Lizzie Atchison, Miss Addie Douglass.

MAJOR AND SURGEON R A BARR

MUSIC COMMITTEE.

Truman Smith, Chairman; Judge J. W. Bonner, W. C. Kilvington, George McWhirter, John B. DeWitt, Alfred LeVane, J. W. Johnson, Frank Henninger, Leon F. Miller, Mrs. W. D. Haggard Jr., Mrs. L. B. Campbell, Mrs. M. S. Lebeck, Miss Mary Demoville, Miss Prudie Polk, Miss Elizabeth Price, Miss Ada Morrow, Miss Nannie Dudley Pilcher, Miss Susie Porterfield.

ENTERTAINMENT COMMITTEE.

S. A. Champion, Chairman; Judge J. M. Anderson, Dr. Rufus Post, Capt. A. J. Harris, T. O. Morris, Nathan Cohn, John Hitchcock, Dr. George H. Price, Wm. Gerst, E. A. Price, Thos. J. Tyne, Andrew Milton, John A. Demoville, R. F. Moore, Tip Gamble, J. W. Baker.

CARRIAGE COMMITTEE.

John C. Brown, Chairman; James A. Ryan, James Grundy, M. S. Lebeck, Robert Currey, O. G. Hills.

PRINTING COMMITTEE.

G. H. Baskette, Chairman; Rev. Ira Landrith, Beau Fitch, A. V. S. Lindsley, John W. Hunter, R. A. Henry, H. M. Meeks, Thomas Goodall.

BADGE COMMITTEE.

Thos. Cooley, Chairman; A. H. Wharton, Dr. W. A. Cheatham, Capt. H. J. Cheny, Samuel Barger, J. Matt Williams, Charles Eastman Jr., A. G. Brandon.

SOUVENIR PROGRAMME COMMITTEE.

G. H. Baskette, Chairman; B. C. Lewis, Jo Frank, compiler and editor, Will T. Hale.

CLARKSVILLE EXECUTIVE COMMITTEE.

Julian F. Gracey, Chairman; Judge C. B. Bailey, Maj. Clay Stacker, Capt. A. F. Smith, T. D. Lockett, H. T. Drane, George Perkins, Mrs. A. F. Smith, Mrs. George Warfield, Mrs. Clay Stacker.

LIEUT. FRANK, BLAKEMORE.

LIEUT. WILLIAM CARUTHERS

CAPT. SPARKMAN AND CAPT. BATES

www.ingramcontent.com/pod-product-compliance
Lightning Source LLC
Chambersburg PA
CBHW031758090426
42739CB00008B/1071